INTRODUCING
ISSUES WITH
OPPOSING
VIEWPOINTS®

Abortion

Noël Merino, *Book Editor*

GREENHAVEN PRESS
A part of Gale, Cengage Learning

GALE
CENGAGE Learning·

Detroit • New York • San Francisco • New Haven, Conn • Waterville, Maine • London

Elizabeth Des Chenes, *Director, Publishing Solutions*

For more information, contact:
Greenhaven Press
27500 Drake Rd.
Farmington Hills, MI 48331-3535
Or you can visit our Internet site at gale.cengage.com

For product information and technology assistance, contact us at

Gale Customer Support, 1-800-877-4253
For permission to use material from this text or product, submit all requests online at
www.cengage.com/permissions

Further permissions questions can be e-mailed to permissionrequest@cengage.com

Articles in Greenhaven Press anthologies are often edited for length to meet page requirements. In addition, original titles of these works are changed to clearly present the main thesis and to explicitly indicate the author's opinion. Every effort is made to ensure that Greenhaven Press accurately reflects the original intent of the authors. Every effort has been made to trace the owners of copyrighted material.

Cover image © Alexander Raths/Shutterstock.com.

LIBRARY OF CONGRESS CATALOGING-IN-PUBLICATION DATA

Abortion / Noël Merino, book editor.
    p. cm. -- (Introducing issues with opposing viewpoints)
  Includes bibliographical references and index.
  ISBN 978-0-7377-5670-8 (hbk.)
  1. Abortion. 2. Abortion--Law and legislation. 3. Abortion--Social aspects. I. Merino, Noël.
  HQ767.A1534 2012
  362.19'888--dc23

2011047672

Printed in the United States of America
2 3 4 5 6 7 16 15 14 13 12

Contents

Chapter 3: Does Legal Abortion Benefit or Harm Society?

Foreword

I ndulging in a wide spectrum of ideas, beliefs, and perspectives is a critical cornerstone of democracy. After all, it is often debates over differences of opinion, such as whether to legalize abortion, how to treat prisoners, or when to enact the death penalty, that shape our society and drive it forward. Such diversity of thought is frequently regarded as the hallmark of a healthy and civilized culture. As the Reverend Clifford Schutjer of the First Congregational Church in Mansfield, Ohio, declared in a 2001 sermon, "Surrounding oneself with only like-minded people, restricting what we listen to or read only to what we find agreeable is irresponsible. Refusing to entertain doubts once we make up our minds is a subtle but deadly form of arrogance." With this advice in mind, Introducing Issues with Opposing Viewpoints books aim to open readers' minds to the critically divergent views that comprise our world's most important debates.

Introducing Issues with Opposing Viewpoints simplifies for students the enormous and often overwhelming mass of material now available via print and electronic media. Collected in every volume is an array of opinions that captures the essence of a particular controversy or topic. Introducing Issues with Opposing Viewpoints books embody the spirit of nineteenth-century journalist Charles A. Dana's axiom: "Fight for your opinions, but do not believe that they contain the whole truth, or the only truth." Absorbing such contrasting opinions teaches students to analyze the strength of an argument and compare it to its opposition. From this process readers can inform and strengthen their own opinions, or be exposed to new information that will change their minds. Introducing Issues with Opposing Viewpoints is a mosaic of different voices. The authors are statesmen, pundits, academics, journalists, corporations, and ordinary people who have felt compelled to share their experiences and ideas in a public forum. Their words have been collected from newspapers, journals, books, speeches, interviews, and the Internet, the fastest growing body of opinionated material in the world.

Introducing Issues with Opposing Viewpoints shares many of the well-known features of its critically acclaimed parent series, Opposing Viewpoints. The articles are presented in a pro/con format, allowing readers to absorb divergent perspectives side by side. Active reading questions preface each viewpoint, requiring the student to approach the material thoughtfully and carefully. Useful charts, graphs, and cartoons supplement each article. A thorough introduction provides readers with crucial background on an issue. An annotated bibliography points the reader toward articles, books, and websites that contain additional information on the topic. An appendix of organizations to contact contains a wide variety of charities, nonprofit organizations, political groups, and private enterprises that each hold a position on the issue at hand. Finally, a comprehensive index allows readers to locate content quickly and efficiently.

Introducing Issues with Opposing Viewpoints is also significantly different from Opposing Viewpoints. As the series title implies, its presentation will help introduce students to the concept of opposing viewpoints, and learn to use this material to aid in critical writing and debate. The series' four-color, accessible format makes the books attractive and inviting to readers of all levels. In addition, each viewpoint has been carefully edited to maximize a reader's understanding of the content. Short but thorough viewpoints capture the essence of an argument. A substantial, thought-provoking essay question placed at the end of each viewpoint asks the student to further investigate the issues raised in the viewpoint, compare and contrast two authors' arguments, or consider how one might go about forming an opinion on the topic at hand. Each viewpoint contains sidebars that include at-a-glance information and handy statistics. A Facts About section located in the back of the book further supplies students with relevant facts and figures.

Following in the tradition of the Opposing Viewpoints series, Greenhaven Press continues to provide readers with invaluable exposure to the controversial issues that shape our world. As John Stuart Mill once wrote: "The only way in which a human being can make some approach to knowing the whole of a subject is by hearing what can be said about it by persons of every variety of opinion and studying all modes in which it can be looked at by every character of mind. No wise man ever acquired his wisdom in any mode but this." It is to this principle that Introducing Issues with Opposing Viewpoints books are dedicated.

Introduction

"Of all the sharply debated moral and political issues in America, abortion is the most divisive."

—President Jimmy Carter, *Our Endangered Values: America's Moral Crisis*

Abortion has been one of the most divisive issues in American politics for decades. Despite the fact that abortion in early pregnancy has been constitutionally protected since the US Supreme Court's decision in *Roe v. Wade* in 1973, the controversy about abortion remains. Although there has always been a vocal political debate in the United States about whether *Roe v. Wade* should be overturned, in recent years the debate has shifted to focus more on what kind of restrictions there should be on legal abortion. One of the central issues in this debate about restrictions is government funding of abortion.

Even among some who approve of the legal status of abortion, debate rages about the funding for abortion. In particular, direct or indirect government funding of abortion has always been a polarizing issue. After *Roe v. Wade* was decided, US Representative Henry Hyde sponsored a bill prohibiting the use of federal funds to pay for abortions. Beginning in 1976, the Hyde Amendment has been attached to the annual federal spending bill every year, prohibiting the use of appropriated federal funds within the bill from being used for abortion, with limited exceptions. The exceptions change from year to year depending on the political views of the members of Congress, always including an exception when the pregnant woman's life is at stake and sometimes including other exceptions, such as when pregnancy results from rape and incest.

Since abortion is a medical procedure, many women cover the cost of abortion through their health insurance. For women who have health insurance or medical care through the federal government, however, the Hyde Amendment's restriction on federal funding precludes the use of their federal health care benefits for abortion. This means that low-income women covered by Medicaid, women covered by federal health insurance due to employment by the government, women serving in the military, women in the Peace Corps, women in federal prison, and women receiving health care from Indian Health Services cannot get health coverage if they choose abortion.

Opponents of the Hyde Amendment's restriction on federal funding of abortion argue that such bans on federal funding of abortion are discriminatory and harm women's health. Regarding the ban on using Medicaid for abortion, the American Civil Liberties Union (ACLU) argues that the federal government "should not use its dollars to intrude on a poor woman's decision whether to carry to term or to terminate her pregnancy and selectively withhold benefits because she seeks to exercise her right of reproductive choice in a manner the government disfavors." Low-income women covered by Medicaid can still obtain an abortion as long as they pay for it themselves, but the ACLU argues that for many low-income women abortion is not affordable, so "denying funding compels many women to carry their pregnancies to term." The ACLU contends that the funding restriction unfairly imposes "a particular religious or moral viewpoint on those women who rely on government-funded health care."[1]

The ban on federal funding of abortion for servicewomen covered by health care plans provided by the US military is not a complete bar to obtaining an abortion, as a woman may elect to pay for her abortion on her own. For women serving overseas, however, current law bars them from obtaining an abortion at a military medical facility, even if they use their own funds. Planned Parenthood argues, "The current ban on privately funded abortions in military facilities threatens the health and lives of women serving overseas" since a servicewoman overseas would need to seek out an abortion in a foreign country where "abortion care may be inadequate, unsafe or altogether unavailable—forcing a woman into a dangerous, security-compromised situation."[2] Former assistant secretary of defense Lawrence J. Korb argues that this lack of abortion coverage for servicewomen is "grossly unfair" and urges Congress to pass a bill "allowing servicewomen to use their own funds to obtain abortion care at military health facilities."[3]

Supporters of the Hyde Amendment's restriction on federal funding of abortion argue that such bans on federal funding of abortion are necessary to ensure that taxpayers do not have to fund a procedure with which they disagree. Federal legislative director for the National Right to Life Committee (NRLC) Douglas Johnson argues that the majority of Americans do not want public funds to pay for abortion, citing a 2010 Quinnipiac University poll finding that 67 percent of Americans feel this way. Johnson says, "The Hyde Amendment has proven itself to be the greatest domestic abortion-reduction law ever enacted by Congress,"[4] but nonetheless argues it does not go far enough in ensuring that federal funds do not pay for abortion, urging Congress to pass legislation strengthening the ban on taxpayer funding of abortion.

Opponents of lifting the ban on providing abortion at military bases argue that the ban actually protects women. US Army officer Joey Hendrix worries that "allowing military facilities to provide abortions would give military leaders the opportunity to put pressure on soldiers when pregnancy interferes, or appears to interfere, with mission goals." Expressing the opposite worry of those who claim that the ban pressures women to proceed with pregnancy, Hendrix claims that "repealing the ban might end up encouraging abortions, because female soldiers would face implicit, or even explicit, pressure to put the mission ahead of their pregnancy."[5] Former US Army officer Jody Duffy expresses concern that "providing abortions on military bases would put many [pregnant service women] at risk of suffering post-abortion stress disorder,"[6] thus harming the military's effectiveness.

The debate about abortion in America is likely to continue for some time. From the disagreement about the Supreme Court's decision in *Roe v. Wade*, to arguments about the morality of abortion, to concerns about women's rights, this divisive issue offers little hope of consensus. Diverse opinions on some of the most contentious issues about abortion are explored in *Introducing Issues with Opposing Viewpoints: Abortion.*

Notes

1. American Civil Liberties Union, "Public Funding for Abortion," July 21, 2004. www.aclu.org/reproductive-freedom/public-funding -abortion.
2. Planned Parenthood, "Planned Parenthood Applauds Senate Committee Vote to Repeal Ban on Privately Funded Abortion Care for Servicewomen," May 28, 2010. www.plannedparenthood.org/about -us/newsroom/press-releases/planned-parenthood-applauds-senate

-cornmittee-vote-repeal-ban-privately-funded-abortion-care-ser
-32721.htm.

3. Lawrence J. Korb, "US Military's Abortion Policy Is Out of Date," *Los Angeles Times*, June 30, 2011. http://articles.latimes.com /2011/jun/30/opinion/la-oe-korb-abortion-20110630.

4. Douglas Johnson, testimony before the Subcommittee on Health, Committee on Energy and Commerce, US House of Representatives, February 9, 2011. www.nrlc.org/AHC/Protect LifeActDouglas JohnsonTestimony.pdf.

5. Joey Hendrix, "Abortions for Soldiers at US Military Bases?," *Christian Science Monitor*, July 21, 2010. www.csmonitor.com /Commentary/Opinion/2010/0721/Abortions-for-soldiers-at-US -military-bases.

6. Jody Duffy, "Abortion: Keep Our Military Abortion-Free," *Los Angeles Times*, July 7, 2011. http://opinion.latimes.com/opinionla /2011/07/abortion-keep-our-military-abortion-free-blowback.html.

Chapter 1

Is Abortion Immoral?

Whether pro-life or pro-choice, each side of the controversial abortion issue thinks its stance is morally supportable.

Viewpoint 1

Abortion Is Unjustified Homicide

Matthew Flannagan

"Feticide constitutes unjustified homicide, and, hence, should not be a practice that is tolerated or sanctioned by the state."

In the following viewpoint Matthew Flannagan argues that abortion, or feticide (the killing of a fetus), is homicide—the killing of a human being—and that it is consequently immoral. Flannagan denies that the fact that a fetus is inside a woman justifies abortion. Furthermore, he claims that the prevention of back-alley abortions and the prevention of unwanted children cannot justify homicide. Flannagan is a theologian in New Zealand.

AS YOU READ, CONSIDER THE FOLLOWING QUESTIONS:
1. What three examples does Flannagan give of things women do not have a right to use their bodies to do?
2. The author claims that what percentage of abortions are done because of a threat to the woman's life or pregnancies that result from rape?
3. What is one of the examples Flannagan uses to argue that lack of consciousness is not required for status as a human being?

Matthew Flannagan, "Confessions of an Anti–Choice Fanatic," *Investigate*, vol. 9, January 2010, pp. 26–27.

I f current media is to be believed, opposition to legal abortion comes from misogynist fundamentalist fanatics who want to impose their religious mores onto others. This string of pejorative terms is amusing; however, it does not actually address the more crucial question of whether laws against feticide (the killing of a fetus) are just. I maintain they are and, unlike most media commentators and politicians who pontificate on the topic, I will argue three points for this thesis.

The Right to Control One's Body

The first is that the typical arguments in favour of abortion succeed only if it is assumed from the outset that feticide is not a form of homicide. A couple of examples will illustrate this. It is frequently asserted that women have a right to do whatever they like with their own bodies. This assertion is false. Women do not have a right to do whatever they like with their bodies; no one has such a right. Women cannot use their bodies to rape or commit homicide or set fires. The right to do as we please is limited by the morality of our actions, thus whether abortion falls into the category of an action we are free to choose depends on whether feticide is homicide. If it is, then this argument fails but as currently used it is just "assumed" that it is not.

Some might object that such an interpretation is an uncharitable reading of this contention. What is important from this perspective is that all people have a right to control what happens inside or to their own bodies. I have a right to control what happens to mine and you have a right to control what happens to yours. Hence, provided the decision I make does not involve me using your body in a way that you do not consent to then I have a right to do it. However, implicit in this argument is the claim that a fetus, at least until born, is part of a woman's body, that it is not a separate, bodily-living, human being on its own. However, this claim is erroneous. To suggest that a fetus is part of a woman's body entails that the mother of a male fetus has two heads, four arms and a penis. Once again this argument is successful only if one assumes a fetus is not a human being from the outset because if the fetus is human then it too has a right to not have its body harmed.

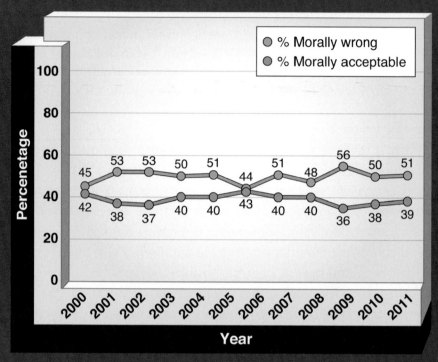

Americans' Views on the Morality of Abortion

○ % Morally wrong
○ % Morally acceptable

Percenetage

100
80
60
40
20
0

45 53 53 50 51   51   48   56 50 51
42 38 37 40 40 44 43 40 40 36 38 39

2000 2001 2002 2003 2004 2005 2006 2007 2008 2009 2010 2011

Year

Taken from: Lydia Saad, "Americans Still Split Along 'Pro-Choice,' 'Pro-Life' Lines," Gallup Poll, May 23, 2011.

Justifications for Feticide

The infamous illegal "back-street" abortion argument fares no better. The allegation that "hundreds" (I put this in scare-quotes because actually the figures show it was significantly a lot less than this) of women died from illegal abortions can justify legalisation only if feticide is not homicide. If it is homicide then this argument reduces to the bizarre assertion that we should kill eighteen thousand children [in New Zealand] each year in order to prevent "hundreds" of women from harming themselves by breaking the law.

Typical consequentialist arguments also fail. Abortion prevents unwanted children who are likely to be poor, abused or engage in crime. It is hailed as a solution to over-population and the existence of more handicapped people. It prevents adult and teenage women from falling into economic hardship and stress. It enables them to complete their education, pursue their careers. However, all this is equally true of infanticide [killing of infants]. Infanticide prevents the existence of unwanted children and their associated social costs, lowers the population, prevents the handicapped existing and saves women and teenagers from the economic and emotional stresses of parenthood. Yet infanticide, as convenient as it is, is condemned because it is homicide. So you can see that, again, all these arguments assume that the fetus is not human without actually arguing for it.

Many antiabortionists argue that abortion is feticide, or murder, and therefore unjustified in all but the rarest cases.

Reasons for Thinking Feticide Is Homicide

This is not to say feticide can never be justified. Utilising the justification of self-defence, I think a case can be made for feticide where pregnancy constitutes a threat to a woman's life or perhaps in cases of rape. Such cases are extremely rare and make up less than 0.5% of all cases [in New Zealand]. So, if feticide is homicide, the vast majority of abortions lack justification. To defend permissive abortion laws on these grounds is a bit like allowing people to murder on demand on the grounds that there exist rare cases of justifiable killing in self-defence.

My second point is [that] the claim that feticide is homicide has considerable prima facie [at first sight] plausibility. Consider this scenario. A hunter is in the woods and notices some rustling in the bushes. Looking through his scope he sees a six-foot-high, bipedal [two-legged] being with brown hair, blue eyes, wearing a swann-dri [an outdoor shirt]. He refrains from shooting. Here, the hunter makes the sensible and reasonable judgment that in firing he would risk engaging in homicide. He bases this on what the target looked like. In the absence of reasons for thinking otherwise he has good grounds for this claim. However, [according to philosopher David Boonin,] "[there is] a general consensus that the fetus is recognisably human after six weeks, and certainly after eight. This fact, conjoined with the above illustration, entails that, in the absence of good reasons to the contrary there are good grounds for thinking that feticide is homicide.

Reasons to Doubt That Fetuses Are Human

My final point is that good reasons to the contrary are not forthcoming. Here I will focus on three common examples starting with the fetus not being viable.

The fact that a fetus cannot survive independently of its mother does not mean it is not a human being. Fetal viability is contingent upon the medical technology of a given culture. A fetus that is not viable in Chad is viable in Los Angeles. If viability is necessary for something to be a human then a woman pregnant with a viable fetus in Los Angeles who flies from Los Angeles to Chad carries a human being when she leaves but this human being ceases to exist when she arrives in Africa and yet becomes human again when she returns.

Similarly, while the fetus lacks consciousness, lack of consciousness does not make a being non-human. If it did, then a human being ceases to exist when asleep or unconscious and then pops back into existence upon awakening. Shooting someone would cease to be homicide provided we render him or her unconscious first. . . .

In summation, except for a few rare cases, abortion is justified only if feticide is not homicide. However, there are good prima facie grounds for thinking feticide is homicide and these prima facie grounds are not overridden by reasons to the contrary. Jointly, these contentions demonstrate that feticide constitutes unjustified homicide, and, hence, should not be a practice that is tolerated or sanctioned by the state.

EVALUATING THE AUTHOR'S ARGUMENTS:

In this viewpoint Matthew Flannagan contends that abortion is an unjustified killing of a human being. What arguments would William Saletan, author of the following viewpoint, present to dispute Flannagan's position?

Abortion Does Not Have the Moral Status of Murder

William Saletan

> *"Is abortion murder? Or is it something less . . . ? Most of us think it's the latter.*

In the following viewpoint William Saletan argues that abortion is not murder. Saletan claims that even people who are pro-life do not really believe that abortion is murder. To prove his point, Saletan argues that if abortion had the moral status of murder, then in a society without laws to protect the unborn the assassination of abortion doctors would be justified —even praiseworthy. But, Saletan concludes, only a handful of extremists hold such a view, thus proving that people do not really believe that abortion is murder even when they say they do. Saletan is *Slate*'s national correspondent and the author of *Bearing Right: How Conservatives Won the Abortion War.*

AS YOU READ, CONSIDER THE FOLLOWING QUESTIONS:
  1. The author claims that George Tiller was one of what two kinds of abortion providers, depending on one's viewpoint?
  2. According to Saletan, how did the nation's leading pro-life group react to the assassination of George Tiller?
  3. Evidence that pro-life groups do not actually believe abortion is murder is that there is not a single proposed piece of legislation to do what, according to Saletan?

If abortion is murder, the most efficient thing you could have done to prevent such murders this month was to kill George Tiller [who was murdered May 31, 2009]. Tiller was the country's bravest or most ruthless abortion provider, depending on how you saw him. The pregnancies he ended were the latest of the late. If your local clinic said you were too far along, and they sent you to a late-term provider who said you were too late even for her, Tiller was your last shot. If Tiller said no, you were going to have a baby, or a dying baby, or a stillbirth, or whatever nature and circumstance had in store for you.

To me, Tiller was brave. His work makes me want to puke. But so does combat, the kind where guts are spilled and people choke on their own blood. I like to think I love my country and would fight for it. But I doubt I have the stomach to pull the trigger, much less put my life on the line.

Several years ago, I went to a conference of abortionists. Some of the late-term providers were there. A row of tables displayed forceps for sale. They started small and got bigger and bigger. Walking along the row, you could ask yourself: Would I use these forceps? How about those? Where would I stop?

The people who do late-term abortions are the ones who don't flinch. They're like the veterans you sometimes see in war documentaries, quietly recounting what they faced and did. You think you're pro-choice. You think marching or phone-banking makes you an activist. You know nothing. There's you, and then there are the people who work in the clinics. And then there are the people who use the forceps. And then there are the people who use the forceps nobody else will use. At the end of the line, there's George Tiller. Now he's gone. Who will pick up his forceps?

Physician George Tiller (pictured), an abortion provider, was murdered by an antiabortion activist in May 2009.

The Logic of Killing Abortion Providers

Tiller's murder is different from all previous murders of abortion providers. If you kill an ordinary abortionist, somebody else will step in. But if you kill the guy at the end of the line, some of his patients won't be able to find an alternative. You will have directly prevented abortions.

That seems to be what Tiller's alleged assassin, Scott Roeder, had in mind. According to the *Washington Post*, Roeder told other pro-lifers that he condoned deadly violence to stop abortions. He admired the Army of God's "Defensive Action Statement," which endorses the murder of abortion providers on the grounds that "whatever force is legitimate to defend the life of a born child is legitimate to defend the life of an unborn child."

Is that statement wrong? Is it wrong to defend the life of an unborn child as you would defend the life of a born child? Because that's the question this murder poses. Peaceful pro-lifers have already tried to prosecute Tiller for doing late-term abortions they claimed were against the law. They failed to convict him. If unborn children are morally equal to born children, then Tiller's assassin has just succeeded where the legal system failed: He has stopped a mass murderer from killing again.

So is Roeder getting support from the nation's leading pro-life groups? Not a bit. They have roundly denounced the murder. The National Right to Life Committee says it opposes "any form of violence to fight the violence of abortion," preferring instead "to work through educational and legislative activities to ensure the right to life for unborn children, people with disabilities and older people." Americans United for Life agrees that it was wrong to kill Tiller because "the foundational right to life that our work is dedicated to extends to everyone."

I applaud these statements. They affirm the value of life and nonviolence, two principles that should unite us. But they don't square with what these organizations purport to espouse: a strict moral equation between the unborn and the born. If a doctor in Kansas were butchering hundreds of old or disabled people, and legal authorities failed to intervene, I doubt most members of the National Right to Life Committee would stand by waiting for "educational and legislative activities" to stop him. Somebody would use force.

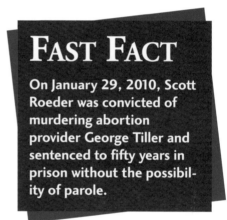

FAST FACT

On January 29, 2010, Scott Roeder was convicted of murdering abortion provider George Tiller and sentenced to fifty years in prison without the possibility of parole.

Abortionists and Murderers

The reason these pro-life groups have held their fire, both rhetorically and literally, is that they don't really equate fetuses with old or disabled people. They oppose abortion, as most of us do. But they don't treat abortionists the way they'd treat mass murderers of the old or disabled. And this self-restraint can't simply be chalked up to nonviolence or respect for the law. Look up the bills these organizations have written, pushed, or passed to restrict abortions. I challenge you to find a single bill that treats a woman who procures an abortion as a murderer. They don't even propose that she go to jail.

The people who kill abortion providers are the ones who don't flinch. They're like the veterans you sometimes see in war documentaries, quietly recounting what they faced and did. You think you're pro-life. You tell yourself that abortion is murder. Maybe you even say that when a pollster calls. But like most of the other people who say such things in polls, you don't mean it literally. There's you, and then there are the people who lock arms outside the clinics. And then there are the people who bomb them. And at the end of the line, there's the guy who killed George Tiller.

If you don't accept what he did, then maybe it's time to ask yourself what you really believe. Is abortion murder? Or is it something less, a tragedy that would be better avoided? Most of us think it's the latter. We're looking for ways to prevent abortions—not just a few this month, but millions down the line—without killing or prosecuting people. Come and join us.

EVALUATING THE AUTHOR'S ARGUMENTS:

In this viewpoint William Saletan proposes that if one supports the view that abortion is murder, one must support the view that a woman who gets an abortion is a murderer and should be punished accordingly. Are there any authors in this chapter who would support such a view of women who get abortions? Explain your answer.

Abortion Violates the Right to Life of the Unborn Baby

"[Abortion] violates the most fundamental human right, the right to life."

Frank Pavone

In the following viewpoint Frank Pavone contends that there is no room for simply "agreeing to disagree" when it comes to abortion. Pavone claims that those in the pro-life movement believe that abortion violates a fundamental human right to life. Thus, he claims it is inconceivable to stop defending the rights of the unborn. Furthermore, the author claims that just because abortion is legal does not mean it is a settled issue, pointing to previous American laws based on error. Pavone is national director of Priests for Life and president of the National Pro-life Religious Council.

AS YOU READ, CONSIDER THE FOLLOWING QUESTIONS:

1. According to the author, what two pro-life politicians have suggested a truce on abortion?
2. Pavone claims that the posture of "agree to disagree" is not neutral because it neutralizes what?
3. In what case, according to the author, did the Supreme Court change its mind about child labor?

I t is dismaying to hear some pro-life politicians calling for a "truce" on social issues like abortion—possible White House contenders Indiana Gov. Mitch Daniels and Mississippi Gov. Haley Barbour among them. Their suggestion is that it's more important to do whatever is necessary to get elected than to worry about issues that appear to be intractable.

This tactic is akin to the pro-life and pro-abortion movements agreeing to disagree, an option often considered a reasonable one. It does not require that either side change its views, but simply agrees to allow the different views, and the practices that flow from them.

There Can Be No Truce

Sorry, but this is a proposal we in the pro-life movement can't accept. There can be no truce. First of all, to ask us to "agree to disagree" about abortion is to ask us to change our position on it. Why do we disagree in the first place? When we oppose abortion, we disagree with the notion that it is even negotiable. We do not only claim that we cannot practice abortion, but that nobody can practice it, precisely because it violates the most fundamental human right, the right to life. To "agree to disagree" means that we no longer see abortion for what it is—a violation of a right so fundamental that disagreement cannot be allowed to tamper with it.

To "agree to disagree" is to foster the notion that the baby is a baby only if the mother thinks it is, that the child has value only if the mother says it does and that we have responsibility only for those we choose to have responsibility for.

Certainly, there are many disputes in our nation about which we can "agree to disagree." Various proposals, programs and strategies can be debated as we try to figure out how best to secure people's rights. But these legitimate areas of disagreement relate to how to secure people's rights, whereas the abortion controversy is about whether to secure or even recognize those rights at all. We can agree to disagree whether certain government programs should be allowed, but not whether acts of violence should be allowed. "Agree to disagree" seems like a neutral posture to assume, but it neutralizes what can never be neutral; namely, the right to life.

A Matter of Justice

Furthermore, the abortion dispute is not merely about conceptual disagreement—it's about justice. It's about violence, bloodshed and victims who need to be defended. In the midst of a policy permitting

The viewpoint author, Father Frank Pavone, conducts a memorial service. An outspoken opponent of abortion, he contends that compromising with the positions of pro-choice advocates is not even an option for pro-life supporters.

thousands of babies a day to be killed, to "agree to disagree" means to cease to defend the absolute rights of these victims.

We don't fight oppression by "agreeing to disagree" with the oppressor. It is precisely when the oppressor disagrees that we have to intervene to stop the violence. The fact that the oppressor does not recognize the victim as a person does not remove our obligation to the victim. In the face of injustice, we are not simply called to disagree with it, but to stop it.

Worse even than the notion of agreeing to disagree is the suggestion that abortion is irrelevant as an issue in the 2010 elections because it is "settled law." No issue is less settled than abortion. More importantly, America's courts and legislatures have a history of changing "settled law."

Dred Scott v. Sandford (1856) is the most commonly cited instance. The slaveholder's right to property eclipsed and subsumed the slave's right to freedom. But the Constitution eventually was amended to correct the error.

Decisions like *Lochner v. New York* (1905) show us another error: Employers' right to contract eclipsed and subsumed the workers' rights to humane conditions and hours. These abuses were corrected by subsequent Supreme Court decisions like *Muller v. Oregon* and *Bunting v. Oregon*.

The "separate but equal" doctrine of *Plessy v. Ferguson* (1896) sanctioning segregation was overturned by *Brown v. Board of Education* some 58 years later.

Erroneous decisions like *Hammer v. Dagenhart* (1918) institutionalized child labor. But this was overturned 23 years later by *United States v. Darby*. A new development—a "pedagogical moment"—occurred here in constitutional law. The question was whether constitutional rights applied to children, too. The answer was yes.

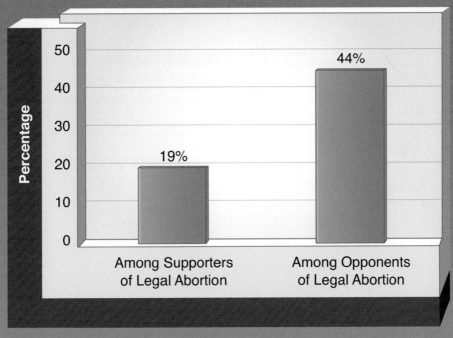

Americans Who Believe There Is No Room for Compromise on the Issue of Abortion

Taken from: Pew Forum on Religion & Public Life, "2009 Annual Religion and Public Life Survey," 2009.

Many reversals of Supreme Court cases came about when new evidence made it clear that someone's rights, not previously recognized, were being violated. Thus, [Supreme Court justice] Louis Brandeis brought forward the facts about how workers were being harmed.

We are now witnessing the same trend regarding children in the womb. Evidence that has been around for quite some time demonstrating their humanity, and their inalienable right to life, is finding its way into legislatures and courts.

With hundreds of embryological studies, and massive evidence of the harm abortion does to women, such evidence, combined with new legal concepts, can challenge *Roe v. Wade* in the same way its erroneous ancestral decisions were challenged.

The day after *Roe v. Wade* was decided, the *New York Times* headline read, "Supreme Court settles abortion." It has remained the most unsettled issue on our national landscape.

EVALUATING THE AUTHOR'S ARGUMENTS:

In this viewpoint Frank Pavone refers to the absolute rights of fetuses. In what way would Karen Espíndola, author of the following viewpoint, take issue with the idea that the fetus's rights are absolute?

Prohibition on Abortion Violates the Human Rights of Women

Karen Espíndola

"Abortion . . . really is a matter of human rights."

In the following viewpoint Karen Espíndola argues that it is a violation of human rights to prohibit abortion. Espíndola recounts her experience in requesting therapeutic abortion in Chile, where abortion is prohibited. She argues that, at minimum, women who find out that their fetus is seriously deformed should be allowed to get therapeutic abortions. She contends that disallowing therapeutic abortion for women who request it is not pro-life because it does not protect the health and human rights of the woman. Espíndola resides in Chile where she is an activist for the rights of women.

AS YOU READ, CONSIDER THE FOLLOWING QUESTIONS:
1. Espíndola mentions what right of children in support of women's right to abortion?
2. The author contends that women should decide whether to become mothers based on what three things?
3. What double standard does Espíndola claim operates in Chile with respect to access to abortion?

When I first found out what could happen during my pregnancy, I went to many different people for help. I felt that a therapeutic abortion was a fair and necessary resolution. Above all, I told the members of [Chile's] Parliament with whom I spoke that denying access to the procedure was a form of torture, a violence that was endured by many women such as myself who were pregnant with fetuses suffering serious malformations, and so this was a problem for the whole country, but very few of them supported me. Most of them try to avoid the issue of abortion. I think that they are trying to ignore the realities of abortion for religious or moral or political reasons, but this really is a matter of human rights.

The Time to Talk About Abortion

However, many more people are in favor of abortion than one might think. They just don't state their position in public, which makes sense since there is so much social repression and punishment for abortion. That is why I have talked about my experiences and the experiences of other women whom I have met in recent months. Many of them do not dare to speak out publicly.

I think that we need to build awareness about the fact that women, even Catholic women, can be in favor of therapeutic abortion. And I myself am open to abortion for other reasons. Children have the right to be wanted, and a woman who has ten children, for example, is unlikely to want or be able to afford another. We cannot turn a blind eye to the impact of poverty and unemployment. . . . How would she be able to feed another child?

In this regard, when you hear a member of Parliament say that "now is not the time to talk about abortion," I say that they are wrong. Now is the time, it is always the time. I call on the President of Chile and her Ministers of State to take a stand on the issue. For example, no one from SERNAM, the Women's Service, has contacted me, and I think that this silence is totally incoherent [with the government's political orientation]. They didn't help me when I was pregnant, and they are not helping me now. I am appealing to them because I think that they are not doing their duty. They owe the people.

Countries That Prohibit Abortion

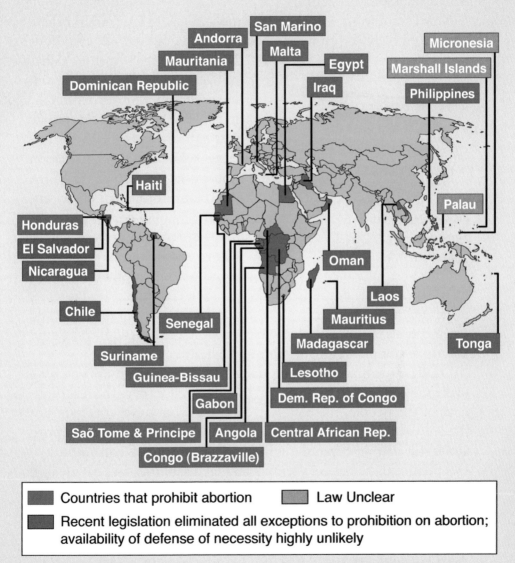

Countries that prohibit abortion

Law Unclear

Recent legislation eliminated all exceptions to prohibition on abortion; availability of defense of necessity highly unlikely

Taken from: Center for Reproductive Rights, "The World's Abortion Laws," September 2009.

Issues of Health

But I am trying to make sense of my suffering. It changed my life. When I was only 13 weeks pregnant I got a very serious diagnosis and I also knew that there was nothing else to do but wait. My family and I never thought that we were going to encounter such huge obstacles. I got online and looked at all the fora on abortion on the Internet, I read everything that I could find and I realized that in Chile, even the debate on abortion is criminalized.

Now I want to stress that I am Catholic, I talk to God, and I believe that the problem is with those who are interpreting God's Word. I don't think that I am a sinner for thinking this way. I just don't identify with the totally repressive discourse of the priests. I think that God didn't make these restrictive laws, this terrible suffering. I also think that the decision should be in women's hands. When the fetal malformations are so serious, they should be able to terminate the pregnancy, in other words, women should decide whether or not to become mothers based on their own individual realities, their lives, their conditions. In this sense, therapeutic abortion is necessary because it also relieves your mental health; a tremendous trauma will always be present in my life and this situation affects my comprehensive health and the health of my family.

FAST FACT

In over thirty countries, including Ireland and Mexico, abortion is allowed only to save the pregnant woman's life.

I really hope that society responds to my demands, that those who make the laws give me an answer, that they reflect over the real problems of the people, the common folk who vote for them. I am not the only woman who has had a diagnosis like this. My child was born and is still alive and even though his disability is not as bad as the doctors predicted, he has very serious mental disabilities and his medical expenses will always be extremely high. So I am asking those who make the laws and those who govern our nation to help me be able to take care of him and to also provide me with mental health care.

A Matter of Human Rights

I really think that the situation is very hypocritical. We talk a lot about life, about protecting life, but in truth, our society is not like that at all. There is a double standard that is seen in the expensive clinics where illegal but safe abortions are performed, while women with fewer resources risk their lives or must bear unwanted pregnancies to term. I think that in our country, we must change people's minds, starting with the young people and working our way up. The powers that be really control the situation and the military regime still somehow continues to be present in an authoritarianism that imposes its ideas and values, which we don't all share but are forced to obey.

I insist, it is matter of human rights, and the entire process that I have experienced—being diagnosed, requesting the abortion, knocking on so many doors, being harassed by the media and the anti-abortion groups

Women belonging to Chilean proabortion and human rights groups demonstrate in Santiago, Chile, for a woman's right to choose. Abortion is illegal in Chile, where an estimated 160,000 to 200,000 illegal abortions are performed annually.

until my son was born—this whole process has been very hard, very difficult. Now, today in Chile abortion is an issue on the debate because of the upcoming elections. Well, I think that this is an important step forward, but more than debating because of the context of the nation's political scene, I would ask that the legislators make a decision right now, bearing in mind that human rights are at stake, the human rights of women.

> **EVALUATING THE AUTHOR'S ARGUMENTS:**
>
> In this viewpoint Karen Espíndola focuses on the rights of women to make the decision to have an abortion. What do Matthew Flannagan and Frank Pavone, authors of previous viewpoints in this chapter, say about women's rights?

Abortion Is Wrong Because Human Life Begins at Conception

Colleen Carroll Campbell

"*A living human being—not simply a 'clump of cells' or 'potential life'—inhabits the womb of a pregnant woman.*"

In the following viewpoint Colleen Carroll Campbell argues that the existence of human life is all that is needed to gain human rights. She claims that it is a statement of fact that human life begins at conception. Moreover, Campbell argues that the Supreme Court opinion in *Roe v. Wade* (1973) confused the biological question of human life with the moral question of what value life possesses. She concludes that establishing biological human life is all that is necessary to establish such value and entitle one to human rights. Campbell is a newspaper columnist and hosts a television and radio show titled *Faith & Culture*.

Colleen Carroll Campbell, "Abortion Proponents Distort the Meaning of Personhood," *St. Louis (MO) Post-Dispatch*, August 26, 2010. Reproduced with permission of the *St. Louis Post-Dispatch*.

AS YOU READ, CONSIDER THE FOLLOWING QUESTIONS:
  1. What is the wording in the Missouri law that the author claims is uncontroversial?
  2. Campbell claims that in the Supreme Court's 1973 *Roe v. Wade* opinion, Justice Harry Blackmun was unwilling to explicitly answer what question?
  3. The author argues that abortion-rights advocates claim personhood is necessary for what?

After months of unsuccessfully fighting against Senate Bill 793, a new Missouri law that requires clinics to offer ultrasounds and information about fetal development to women seeking abortions, Planned Parenthood officials and their ilk are trying a new tack. They are trading their charge that optional ultrasounds constitute a threat to women's rights—a nonsensical complaint that never got much traction—for the claim that the law rests on religious and philosophical opinions rather than facts.

A Statement of Fact

The complaint hinges on these words in the law: "The life of each human being begins at conception. Abortion will terminate the life of a separate, unique, living human being."

Sounds pretty straightforward right? Wrong, says Paula Gianino, president and CEO [chief executive officer] of Planned Parenthood of the St. Louis Region and Southwest Missouri. As she told the [*Saint Louis (Missouri)*] *Post-Dispatch* recently, "Those are not sentiments that all the world's religions, or all the people in the state, believe in."

Actually, those are not sentiments at all. They are statements of fact. They can be verified by most any embryology textbook, including those written decades ago, when abortion-rights activists still were claiming that "no one knows when life begins." As the 1975 edition of *Medical Embryology* put it, "The development of a human being begins with fertilization, a process by which two highly specialized cells, the spermatozoon from the male and the oocyte from the female, unite to give rise to a new organism, the zygote."

In other words, sperm meets egg and new life begins. It's elementary sex ed, just the sort that Planned Parenthood advocates for every pigtailed tot in the schoolyard. And it's disturbing to hear the local head of Planned Parenthood dismiss this scientific fact as some obscure bit of religious dogma.

A sperm fertilizes an ovum in this illustration. Pro-life advocates argue that a human being is created at the moment of conception.

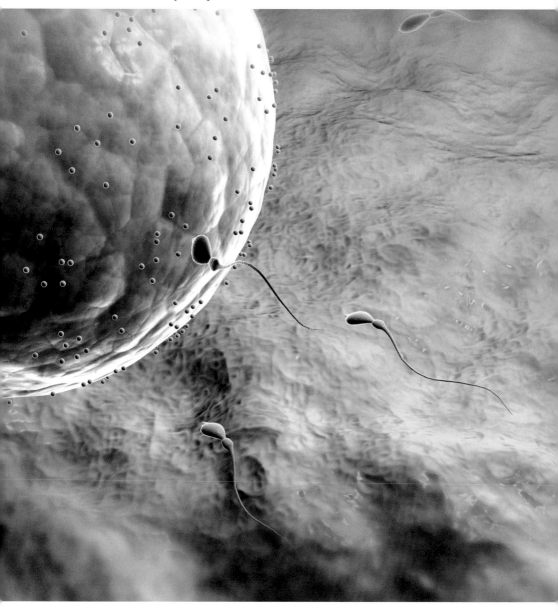

A Biological Question

Of course, such affected ignorance is old news among abortion-rights advocates. In their *Roe v. Wade* ruling of 1973, Supreme Court Justice Harry Blackmun and his colleagues arrogated to themselves the right to overturn anti-abortion laws across America even as they professed no knowledge of a biological fact the average seventh-grader could recite in his sleep.

"We need not resolve the difficult question of when life begins," Blackmun wrote, in a weak attempt to explain why the court had side-stepped the main argument against legalized abortion. "When those trained in the respective disciplines of medicine, philosophy, and theology are unable to arrive at any consensus, the judiciary, at this point in the development of man's knowledge, is not in a position to speculate as to the answer."

"Life-ectomy," cartoon by Gary McCoy and CagleCartoons.com. Copyright © 2007 by Gary McCoy and CagleCartoons.com. All rights reserved. Reproduced by permission.

Blackmun's muddled statement confused the biological question of when human life begins with the moral and philosophical question of what value that nascent human life possesses. Unwilling to explicitly answer the latter, he disingenuously pleaded ignorance about the former.

Abortion-rights activists have been imitating his sleight of hand ever since. Shifting the abortion debate from scientific facts to philosophical theories has become their favorite rhetorical trick now that advances in ultrasound technology have undercut their earlier denials of the unborn child's humanity.

A Human and a Person

Anyone who ever has seen a pair of little hands waving at her from the sonogram screen knows that a living human being—not simply a "clump of cells" or "potential life"—inhabits the womb of a pregnant woman. So abortion-rights advocates now argue that what you see on that sonogram is human and alive but not a human person and, therefore, not entitled to rights.

Exactly what makes a human being a person is unclear. Some abortion-rights advocates define personhood by location—as in, outside the womb—or by such qualities as rationality and autonomy. Using that latter definition, Princeton philosopher Peter Singer argues that severely disabled newborns and demented adults do not count as persons while chimpanzees, gorillas, and orangutans do. Not surprisingly, Singer defends infanticide and euthanasia as well as abortion, claiming that it is illogical to protect human life simply because it is human.

> **FAST FACT**
>
> In *Roe v. Wade* (1973), the US Supreme Court held that states may not implement regulations to protect fetal life until the point of viability, which it said was at the end of the third trimester.

Pro-choice pundits often squirm when Singer starts talking, but he merely follows their favorite new argument to its logical conclusion. If being human is not enough to entitle one to human rights, then the very concept of human rights loses meaning. And all of us—born and unborn, strong and weak, young and old—someday will find ourselves on the wrong end of that cruel measuring stick.

EVALUATING THE AUTHOR'S ARGUMENTS:

In this viewpoint Colleen Carroll Campbell claims that having biological human life is sufficient for having human rights. Why does Garry Wills, author of the following viewpoint, think this is nonsense?

The Existence of Human Life Is Irrelevant to the Moral Issue of Abortion

Garry Wills

> *"The question is not whether the fetus is human life but whether it is a human person, and when it becomes one."*

In the following viewpoint Garry Wills argues that the pro-life movement's focus on human life as morally significant is misguided; rather, he claims, the focus should be on human personhood. Wills argues that there is no religious basis for resolving the abortion issue. He states that being a person is what is morally relevant, not merely being alive and human. Wills concludes that there is much disagreement and uncertainty, which is why the decision is left up to the pregnant woman herself. Wills is the author of numerous books, including *Head and Heart: American Christianities*.

AS YOU READ, CONSIDER THE FOLLOWING QUESTIONS:
1. Whom does Wills claim are the relevant experts on the matter of abortion by natural law?
2. What percentage of abortions has occurred by the end of the second trimester, according to the author?
3. What three entities does Wills reject as being qualified to make the individual decision to have an abortion?

Much of the debate over abortion is based on a misconception—that it is a religious issue, that the pro-life advocates are acting out of religious conviction. It is not a theological matter at all. There is no theological basis for defending or condemning abortion. Even popes have said that the question of abortion is a matter of natural law, to be decided by natural reason. Well, the pope is not the arbiter of natural law. Natural reason is.

Abortion and Religion

John Henry Newman, a 19th century Anglican priest who converted to Catholicism, once wrote that "the pope, who comes of revelation, has no jurisdiction over nature." The matter must be decided by individual conscience, not by religious fiat. As Newman said: "I shall drink to the pope, if you please—still, to conscience first, and to the pope afterward."

If we are to decide the matter of abortion by natural law, that means we must turn to reason and science, the realm of Enlightened religion. But that is just what evangelicals want to avoid. Who are the relevant experts here? They are philosophers, neurobiologists, embryologists. Evangelicals want to exclude them because most give answers they do not want to hear. The experts have only secular expertise, not religious conviction. They, admittedly, do not give one answer—they differ among themselves, they are tentative, they qualify. They do not have the certitude that the religious right accepts as the sign of truth.

Preserving Human Life

So evangelicals take shortcuts. They pin everything on being pro-life. But one cannot be indiscriminately pro-life.

If one claimed, in the manner of [humanitarian and philosopher] Albert Schweitzer, that all life deserved moral respect, then plants have rights, and it might turn out that we would have little if anything to eat. And if one were consistently pro-life, one would have to show moral respect for paramecia, insects, tissue excised during a medical operation, cancer cells, asparagus and so on. Harvesting carrots, on a consistent pro-life hypothesis, would constitute something of a massacre.

Opponents of abortion will say that they are defending only human life. It is certainly true that the fetus is human life. But so is the semen before it fertilizes; so is the ovum before it is fertilized. They are both human products, and both are living things. But not even evangelicals say that the destruction of one or the other would be murder.

Defenders of the fetus say that life begins only after the semen fertilizes the egg, producing an embryo. But, in fact, two-thirds of the embryos produced this way fail to live on because they do not embed in the womb wall. Nature is like fertilization clinics—it produces more embryos than are actually used. Are all the millions of embryos that fail to be embedded human persons?

The universal mandate to preserve "human life" makes no sense. My hair is human life—it is not canine hair, and it is living. It grows. When it grows too long, I have it cut. Is that aborting human life? The same with my growing human fingernails. An evangelical might respond that my hair does not have the potential to become a person.

FAST FACT

Various religious groups, including the Unitarian Universalist Association, United Church of Christ, and United Synagogue of Conservative Judaism, support the right of women to choose abortion.

True. But semen has the potential to become a person, and we do not preserve every bit of semen that is ejaculated but never fertilizes an egg.

The Issue of Personhood

The question is not whether the fetus is human life but whether it is a human person, and when it becomes one. Is it when it is capable of thought, of speech, of recognizing itself as a person, or of assuming

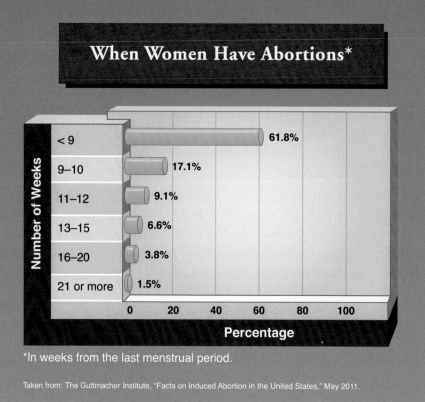

When Women Have Abortions*

Number of Weeks	Percentage
< 9	61.8%
9–10	17.1%
11–12	9.1%
13–15	6.6%
16–20	3.8%
21 or more	1.5%

*In weeks from the last menstrual period.

Taken from: The Guttmacher Institute, "Facts on Induced Abortion in the United States," May 2011.

the responsibilities of a person? Is it when it has a functioning brain? [Medieval theologian Thomas] Aquinas said that the fetus did not become a person until God infused the intellectual soul. A functioning brain is not present in the fetus until the end of the sixth month at the earliest.

Not surprisingly, that is the earliest point of viability, the time when a fetus can successfully survive outside the womb.

Whether through serendipity or through some sort of causal connection, it now seems that the onset of a functioning central nervous system with a functioning cerebral cortex and the onset of viability occur around the same time—the end of the second trimester, a time by which 99% of all abortions have already occurred.

Opponents of abortion like to show sonograms of the fetus reacting to stimuli. But all living cells have electric and automatic reactions. These are like the reactions of Terri Schiavo[1] when she was in a permanent vegetative state. Aquinas, following Aristotle, called the early stage

1. Schiavo, long in a vegetative coma, was the subject of a national controversy in 2005 over whether her life support should be discontinued.

of fetal development vegetative life. The fetus has a face long before it has a brain. It has animation before it has a command center to be aware of its movements or to experience any reaction as pain.

The Individual Decision

These are difficult matters, on which qualified people differ. It is not enough to say that whatever the woman wants should go. She has a responsibility to consider whether and when she may have a child inside her, not just a fetus. Certainly by the late stages of her pregnancy, a child is ready to respond with miraculous celerity to all the personal interchanges with the mother that show a brain in great working order.

Given these uncertainties, who is to make the individual decision to have an abortion? Religious leaders? They have no special authority in the matter, which is not subject to theological norms or guidance. The state? Its authority is given by the people it represents, and the people are divided on this. Doctors? They too differ. The woman is the one closest to the decision. Under *Roe vs. Wade* [the 1973 Supreme Court decision legalizing abortion], no woman is forced to have an abortion. But those who have decided to have one are able to.

EVALUATING THE AUTHOR'S ARGUMENTS:

In this viewpoint Garry Wills suggests that being a human person, not merely having human life, is what is morally important. How does Wills's notion of a human person differ from the concept of a human being put forth by Colleen Carroll Campbell, author of the previous viewpoint?

Chapter 2

Should Abortion Be Legally Restricted?

Antiabortion protesters demonstrate against the US Supreme Court's 1973 decision in Roe v. Wade, *which ruled against states that had determined abortion to be a criminal offense.*

Roe v. Wade Should Be Overturned

Ken Blackwell

"They all know Roe [v. Wade] is wrong."

In the following viewpoint Ken Blackwell argues that the pro-life movement continues to protest the US Supreme Court's ruling in *Roe v. Wade* (1973)—which said a woman's right to abortion was protected by the US Constitution—because they know it is wrong. Blackwell contends that even a renowned liberal law professor agrees that the Court erred in *Roe.* He compares the movement against abortion to the civil rights movement and urges the Supreme Court to overturn its decision in *Roe.* Blackwell is a columnist for the *New York Sun* and is the Senior Fellow for Family Empowerment at the Family Research Council.

AS YOU READ, CONSIDER THE FOLLOWING QUESTIONS:
1. What is one way in which the author claims that the pro-life movement is diverse?
2. What bumper sticker does Blackwell call "morally bankrupt"?
3. Blackwell claims that pro-life protesters are marching in the footsteps of what civil rights leader?

Tens of thousands of pro-lifers will descend upon the streets of Washington, D.C. today [January 22, 2010]. They will come this year—as they have come every year since 1974. It won't matter if there's a "wintry mix." In 1985, the Inauguration of a President was forced indoors for the first time in history. An arctic blast forced cancellation of the Inaugural Parade. But two days later, with frigid winds unabated in their fury, the March for Life went on as scheduled.

They come to bear witness. They come to protest a grave injustice. Some young people have grown up coming every year to this March for Life. Thousands of young people will camp out Thursday night at the Shrine of the Immaculate Conception and attend Mass early on Friday morning. Thousands of others will attend worship services at area Evangelical and Lutheran churches.

The Pro-Life Movement

No cause since the great Civil Rights movement of the 1960s has brought together such a diverse group of supporters. Every race of mankind is represented. Every continent has sent its representatives.

FAST FACT

There are over a million abortions performed each year in the United States.

The pro-life movement has battered down the walls of ancient prejudice separating Catholic from Protestant, and Protestants from other Protestants. Marchers will also hear the sounds of an ancient Hebrew shofar—the ceremonial ram's horn that alerted God's people as far back as the Exodus.

You might think that the 2008 elections would have put an end to right-to-lifers' incessant agitation. You would be wrong. Only when America herself is adjourned will you hear the end of the outcry against this most un-American of rulings.

The Supreme Court's Opinion

What does *Roe* [*v. Wade* (1973)] mean? It means that an abortionist can kill an unborn child and we have no right to object. "If you don't like abortion, don't have one," says a morally bankrupt bumper sticker

Author Ken Blackwell (pictured) believes that today's antiabortion movement is comparable to the civil rights movement of the 1960s.

from the other side. How about: "If you don't like slavery, don't own one?"

We've heard a lot about "the Kennedy seat" in the Massachusetts Senate race this week.[1]

I'd like to talk about the Kennedys' friend. Archibald Cox was certainly a liberal. He was certainly an intellectual. You can't be a Harvard Professor without being an intellectual.

---

1. After decades as a Massachusetts senator, longtime liberal and pro-choice Democrat Ted Kennedy retired for health reasons. Republicans hoped to take his seat in the upcoming 2008 election to offset the Democratic majority in the Senate. To almost everyone's surprise, they did.

But when it came to grading the work of that Harvard Law School graduate, Justice Harry Blackmun, Prof. Cox gave the striving jurist a failing grade:

[Blackmun's opinion] fails even to consider what I would suppose to be the most important compelling interest of the State in prohibiting abortion: the interest in maintaining that respect for the paramount sanctity of human life which has always been at the centre of Western civilization, not merely by guarding life itself, however defined, but by safeguarding the penumbra [related, implied rights], whether at the beginning, through some overwhelming disability of mind or body, or at death. . . .

The failure to confront the issue in principled terms leaves the opinion to read like a set of hospital rules and regulations, whose validity is good enough this week but will be destroyed with new statistics upon the medical risks of child-birth and abortion or new advances in providing for the separate existence of a fetus. . . . Neither historian, nor layman, nor lawyer will be persuaded that all the prescriptions of Justice Blackmun are part of the Constitution.

"Just think, if it hadn't been for *Roe v. Wade*—I would be celebrating my 38th birthday," cartoon by Gary Varvel. Gary Varvel Editorial Cartoon is used with the permission of Gary Varvel and Creators Syndicate. All rights reserved.

A Wrong Opinion

Even a liberal, even a Harvard Law Professor, even a friend of the Kennedy family like Archibald Cox knew why *Roe* is wrong. And the marchers know it, too. From the little children holding their moms' hands to the eighty-somethings being wheeled up to the steps of the U.S. Supreme Court: they all know *Roe* is wrong.

I am proud to stand with the protesters. I am proud to live in a country where we can still peaceably assemble and petition our government for redress of wrongs. We are marching in Dr. [Martin Luther] King's footsteps when we do so.

Lincoln said it well: Nothing stamped in the divine image was sent into the world to be trod upon. We believe unborn children are so stamped. We believe every child should be welcomed in life—and protected in law. May God bless the United States and this honorable court. Especially, may He bless the court with the wisdom at long last to do justice.

EVALUATING THE AUTHOR'S ARGUMENTS:

In this viewpoint, Ken Blackwell compares the pro-life movement with the civil rights movement. Considering what is said in the following viewpoint by the Center for Reproductive Rights, how might the pro-choice movement also compare itself with the civil rights movement?

Viewpoint 2

Roe v. Wade Should Not Be Overturned

Center for Reproductive Rights

"It is not a time for our political leaders to divide this nation by turning the clock back on women's human rights."

In the following viewpoint the Center for Reproductive Rights contends that the US Supreme Court's decision in *Roe v. Wade* (1973) had a positive effect on women and should not be reversed. The author claims that the initial 1973 decision strongly protected a woman's right to abortion but says that the right to abortion has been undermined in recent decades, threatening the advances women have made due to the ability to control decisions about childbearing. The Center for Reproductive Rights is an organization that uses the law to advance reproductive freedom as a fundamental human right.

AS YOU READ, CONSIDER THE FOLLOWING QUESTIONS:

1. According to the Center for Reproductive Rights, approximately how many women died per year from illegal abortions prior to *Roe v. Wade?*
2. Which two presidents, according to the Center for Reproductive Rights, played a large role in the backlash against *Roe v. Wade* in the late twentieth century?
3. What 1992 US Supreme Court decision eliminated two of the four pillars of *Roe v. Wade*, according to the author?

Center for Reproductive Rights, "*Roe v. Wade*—Then and Now," July 1, 2007. http://reproductiverights.org.
Copyright © 2007 by Center for Reproductive Rights. All rights reserved. Reproduced by permission.

On January 22, 1973, the United States Supreme Court struck down the State of Texas's criminal abortion laws, finding that the right to decide whether to have a child is a fundamental right guaranteed by the U.S. Constitution. The 7–2 decision in *Roe v. Wade* would have an immediate and profound effect on the lives of American women.

Before *Roe v. Wade*

Before *Roe*, it is estimated [by Willard Cates Jr. and Robert W. Rochat] that "between 200,000 and 1.2 million illegally induced abortions occur[red] annually in the United States." As many as 5,000 to 10,000 women died per year following illegal abortions and many others suffered severe physical and psychological injury.

To prevent women from dying or injuring themselves from unsafe, illegal or self-induced abortions, women's advocates spearheaded campaigns to reverse century-old criminal abortion laws in the decades preceding *Roe*. During the 1960s and 1970s, a movement of medical, public health, legal, religious and women's organizations successfully urged one-third of state legislatures to liberalize their abortion statutes.

Roe v. Wade is a landmark decision that recognized that the right to make childbearing choices is central to women's lives and their ability to participate fully and equally in society. Yet, the Supreme Court's decision in *Roe* was far from radical—it was the logical extension of High Court decisions on the right to privacy dating back to the turn of the century. The decision is grounded in the same reasoning that guarantees our right to refuse medical treatment and the freedom to resist government search and seizure. In finding that the constitutional right to privacy encompasses a woman's right to choose whether or not to continue a pregnancy, the High Court continued a long line of decisions recognizing a right of privacy that protects intimate and personal decisions—including those affecting childrearing, marriage, procreation and the use of contraception—from governmental interference.

The Decision in *Roe v. Wade*

In its 1973 decision in *Roe*, the Supreme Court recognized that a woman's right to decide whether to continue her pregnancy was protected under the constitutional provisions of individual autonomy and privacy. For the first time, *Roe* placed women's reproductive choice alongside other fundamental rights, such as freedom of speech and freedom of religion, by conferring the highest degree of constitutional protection—"strict scrutiny"—to choice.

Finding a need to balance a woman's right to privacy with the state's interest in protecting potential life, the Supreme Court established a trimester framework for evaluating restrictions on abortion. The Court required the state to justify any interference with the abortion decision by showing that it had a "compelling interest" in doing so. Restrictions on abortions performed before fetal viability, that is the period before a fetus can live outside a woman's body, were limited to those that narrowly and precisely promoted real maternal health concerns. After the point of viability, the state was free to ban abortion or take other steps to promote its interest in protecting fetal life. Even after that point, however, the state's interest in the viable fetus must yield to the woman's right to have an abortion to protect her health and life.

Immediately following the *Roe* decision, those who did not want to see women participate equally in society were galvanized. The far right initiated a political onslaught that has resulted in numerous state and federal abortion restrictions and contributed to a changed Supreme Court, ideologically bent on eviscerating *Roe*. The right to choose became the target of not only the religious right, but also right-wing politicians and judges who used the *Roe* decision to attack the "judicial activism" of the Supreme Court and its purported failure to adhere to the text of the Constitution and the "original intent" of its framers. This backlash reached its peak during the three terms of Presidents [Ronald] Reagan and [George H.W.] Bush. Beginning in 1983, the U.S. solicitor general routinely urged the Supreme Court, on behalf of the federal government, to overturn *Roe*. In addition, when appointing Supreme Court justices, Reagan and Bush used opposition to *Roe* as a litmus test. . . .

FAST FACT

Support for *Roe v. Wade* splits along party lines, with three-quarters of Democrats agreeing with the decision and over half of Republicans disagreeing with it.

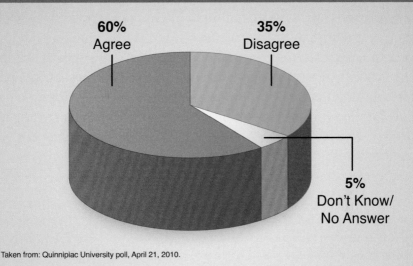

US Opinion on *Roe v. Wade*

Do you agree or disagree with the 1973
***Roe v. Wade* Supreme Court decision?**

60%
Agree

35%
Disagree

5%
Don't Know/
No Answer

Taken from: Quinnipiac University poll, April 21, 2010.

The Dismantling of *Roe v. Wade*

Shortly after the *Roe* decision, state legislatures began passing laws in hopes of creating exceptions to it or opening up areas of law that *Roe* did not directly address. No other right has been frontally attacked and so successfully undermined, and all in the course of two decades—the same two decades that sustained advances in other areas of women's rights, including education and employment. . . .

The *Roe* opinion was grounded on four constitutional pillars: (1) the decision to have an abortion was accorded the highest level of constitutional protection like any other fundamental constitutional right; (2) the government had to stay neutral; legislatures could not enact laws that pushed women to make one decision or another (3) in the period before the fetus is viable, the government may restrict abortion only to protect a woman's health; (4) after viability, the government may prohibit abortion, but laws must make exceptions that permit abortion when necessary to protect a woman's health or life.

Only two of the four *Roe* pillars remain today as a result of the Supreme Court's 1992 decision in *Planned Parenthood of Southeastern Pennsylvania v. Casey.* This decision is the culmination of a steady decline in constitutional protection for the right to privacy. A woman's right to choose is still constitutionally protected; however, the "strict scrutiny" standard was jettisoned in favor of a lesser standard of protection for reproductive choice called "undue burden." Under *Casey*, state and local laws that favor fetal rights and burden a woman's choice to have abortion are permitted, so long as the burden is not "undue." No longer does the state have to be neutral in the choice of abortion or childbearing. Now the government is free to pass laws restricting abortion based on "morality," a code word for religious anti-abortion views. States are now permitted to disfavor abortion and punish women seeking abortions, even those who are young and sick, with harassing laws. . . .

Without *Roe*, life for American women would be thrown more than 30 years in reverse, returning them to the days when women could not

Political activist Phyllis Schlafly speaks to the press, criticizing the 1992 Supreme Court decision in Planned Parenthood of Southeastern Pennsylvania v. Casey, *which failed to overturn* Roe v. Wade.

fully control the number and spacing of their children. Without the ability to make this key decision, women will be denied opportunities to realize their future and take advantage of educational and career opportunities.

The world is looking to the U.S. to establish a vision of justice for the 21st century. It is not a time for our political leaders to divide this nation by turning the clock back on women's human rights.

EVALUATING THE AUTHOR'S ARGUMENTS:

In this viewpoint the Center for Reproductive Rights contends that *Roe v. Wade* has been undermined over the years. What author(s) in this chapter suggest restrictions that the center would see as undermining the Court's 1973 holding in *Roe*?

"The argument that some abortions take place in particularly awful, particularly understandable circumstances is not a case against regulating abortion."

There Should Be Some Restrictions on Abortion

Ross Douthat

In the following viewpoint Ross Douthat argues that the defense of abortion in any case without exception is not reasonable. Douthat claims that supporters of unrestricted abortion use the most extreme examples in support of rejecting all restrictions. He maintains that this results in the support of elective abortion very late in the last trimester, which is extremely controversial. Douthat suggests that the debate be opened up to consider restrictions on abortion not only in the third trimester, but in the second trimester as well. Douthat is an op-ed columnist at the *New York Times*.

AS YOU READ, CONSIDER THE FOLLOWING QUESTIONS:
1. According to Douthat, why was Dr. George Tiller the target of protests?
2. What fraction of abortions in the United States are repeat abortions, according to the author?
3. Douthat claims that under current law what kind of abortion procedures are the only kind that can be disallowed?

The case of [abortion provider] Dr. George Tiller, murdered just over a week ago [on May 31, 2009,] in the lobby of his church, helps explain why so many people believe that abortion should be available at any stage of pregnancy.

The Hardest Cases

Tiller did abortions in the third trimester, when almost no one else would do them—which meant, inevitably, that he handled the hardest of hard cases. He performed abortions on women facing life-threatening complications, on women whose children would be born dead or dying, on women who had been raped, on "women" who were really girls of 10. His Wichita, Kansas, office, barricaded against protesters, was reportedly lined with thank-you notes.

Over the last week, there's been an outpouring of testimonials, across the Internet, from women (and some men) who lived through these hard cases. They help explain why Tiller thought he was doing the Lord's work, even though that work involved destroying something that we wouldn't hesitate to call a baby if we saw it struggling for life in a hospital bed. They help explain why so many Americans defend his right to do it.

> **FAST FACT**
>
> According to the Centers for Disease Control and Prevention, approximately 1 percent of abortions are performed at twenty-one weeks or later (the third trimester starts at twenty-eight weeks).

But such narratives are not the only story about George Tiller's clinic. He was a target of protests—and, tragically, of terrorist violence—because he performed late-term abortions, period. But his critics were convinced that he performed them not only in truly desperate situations, but in many other cases as well. Over the years, they cobbled together a considerable amount of evidence—drawn from the state's abortion statistics, from Tiller's own comments, and from a 2006 investigation—suggesting that Tiller abused the state's mental-health exemption to justify late-term abortions in almost any situation.

A "for sale" sign stands outside physician George Tiller's abortion clinic in Wichita, Kansas. The facility closed after his murder by a pro-life activist.

This evidence is persuasive, but not dispositive. We may never know how many of George Tiller's abortions were performed on healthy mothers and healthy fetuses. But whatever the verdict on Tiller's practice, most abortions in the United States bear no resemblance whatsoever to the hardest third-trimester cases.

The Exceptions and the Rule

Yes, many pregnancies are terminated in dire medical circumstances. But these represent a tiny fraction of the million-plus abortions that take place in the United States every year. (Almost half of that number are repeat abortions; around a quarter are third or fourth procedures.) The same is true of the more than 100,000 abortions that are performed after the first trimester: Very few involve medical complications of any kind. Even the now-outlawed "partial-birth" procedure, which abortion-rights supporters initially argued was only employed in the direst of dire situations, turned out to be used primarily for purely elective abortions.

The argument for unregulated abortion rests on the idea that where there are exceptions, there cannot be a rule. Because rape and incest can lead to pregnancy, because abortion can save women's lives, because babies can be born into suffering and certain death, there should be no restrictions on abortion whatsoever.

As a matter of moral philosophy, this makes a certain sense. Either a fetus has a claim to life or it doesn't. The circumstances of its conception and the state of its health shouldn't enter into the equation.

But the law is a not a philosophy seminar. It's the place where morality meets custom, and compromise, and common sense. And it can take account of tragic situations without universalizing their lessons.

The Need for More Regulation

Indeed, the argument that some abortions take place in particularly awful, particularly understandable circumstances is not a case against regulating abortion. It's the beginning of precisely the kind of reasonable distinction-making that would produce a saner, stricter legal regime.

If anything, by enshrining a near-absolute right to abortion in the Constitution, the pro-choice side has ensured that the hard cases are more controversial than they otherwise would be. One reason there's

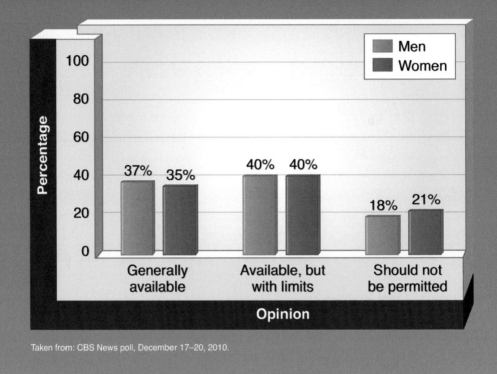

Most Americans Favor Limits on Abortion

Abortion Should be . . .

Men
Women

Percentage

100
80
60
40
20
0

Generally available: Men 37%, Women 35%
Available, but with limits: Men 40%, Women 40%
Should not be permitted: Men 18%, Women 21%

Opinion

Taken from: CBS News poll, December 17–20, 2010.

so much fierce argument about the latest of late-term abortions—
Should there be a health exemption? A fetal deformity exemption?
How broad should those exemptions be?—is that Americans aren't
permitted to debate anything else. Under current law, if you want to
restrict abortion, post-viability procedures are the only kind you're
allowed to even regulate.

If abortion were returned to the democratic process, this landscape
would change dramatically. Arguments about whether and how to restrict
abortions in the second trimester—as many advanced democracies already
do—would replace protests over the scope of third-trimester medical
exemptions.

The result would be laws with more respect for human life, a culture less inflamed by a small number of tragic cases—and a political debate, God willing, unmarred by crimes like George Tiller's murder.

EVALUATING THE AUTHOR'S ARGUMENTS:

In this viewpoint Ross Douthat suggests that a general rule allowing abortion in all cases is not reasonable. Drawing on an argument from another author in this chapter, raise one objection to allowing abortion in some circumstances but not in others.

Restrictions Do Not Significantly Reduce Abortions and Have Harmful Consequences

Janet Pearson

"Measures aimed at dissuading women from having abortions 'do not appear to be effective.'"

In the following viewpoint Janet Pearson contends that continued attempts to implement hurdles to legal abortion are not having any significant impact on abortion rates, but they are harming women. Pearson claims that although the abortion rate has declined in the United States over the last several decades, there is no indication that this is a result of restrictions. Pearson notes that restrictions on surgical abortion have led more women to use the so-called abortion pill. Finally, Pearson claims that the restrictions have had an unnecessarily negative impact on many women in a variety

of ways. Pearson is associate editor at the *Tulsa World,* a daily newspaper in Oklahoma.

AS YOU READ, CONSIDER THE FOLLOWING QUESTIONS:
   1. According to Pearson, how many states regulate abortion-related
      ultrasounds?
   2. What has changed in the US abortion rate from 1980 to 2005,
      according to the author?
   3. The author claims that what countries have the lowest abortion
      rates?

A bortion foes lost a battle last week [August 18, 2009,] in Oklahoma when a judge tossed out a controversial ultrasound
requirement. But that's a minor setback when compared to
the many access-curtailing victories they've scored in recent years.

Concerns About Abortion Restrictions

But have these myriad new measures had the hoped-for effect of reducing the number of abortions performed in the U.S.?

Some new research is, to say the least, unsettling. Abortion restrictions may be fueling huge increases in drug-induced abortions, and
causing women to delay abortions to a riskier point in the pregnancy.
Restrictions also may be increasing the teen birth rate in a few spots.
Most disturbing of all, the new restrictions are disproportionately
impacting low-income and minority women, while higher-income
white women still have little difficulty obtaining abortions.

Surely these are not the sorts of results abortion foes were seeking.

An Oklahoma judge last week ruled against a law that required
women seeking an abortion to receive an ultrasound and doctors to
describe the image.

Oklahoma County District Judge Vicki Robertson determined that
the law—described by advocates as the most extreme of its kind in
the nation—violated the state constitutional requirement that legislative measures deal with only one subject.

Attorney General Drew Edmondson has indicated the state will
appeal Robertson's decision.

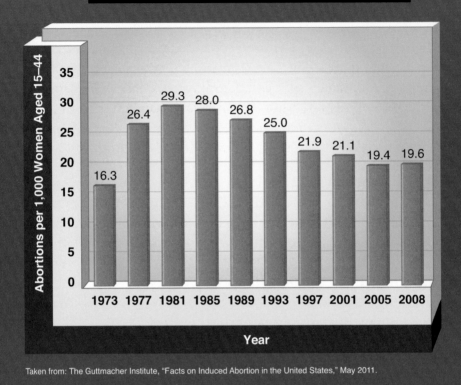

Abortions in the United States, 1973–2008

Abortions per 1,000 Women Aged 15–44

16.3 (1973)
26.4 (1977)
29.3 (1981)
28.0 (1985)
26.8 (1989)
25.0 (1993)
21.9 (1997)
21.1 (2001)
19.4 (2005)
19.6 (2008)

Year

Taken from: The Guttmacher Institute, "Facts on Induced Abortion in the United States," May 2011.

A Variety of Restrictions

Requiring ultrasound procedures before an abortion is a relatively new tactic unabashedly aimed at dissuading women from obtaining abortions. According to the Guttmacher Institute, the nation's leading resource on reproductive data, 13 states regulate abortion-related ultrasounds, but only a few states mandate that an ultrasound be performed before an abortion.

Oklahoma's law was considered the most far-reaching, because it would not only have required an ultrasound prior to an abortion—not always a medical necessity—but also would have directed the provider to describe the images shown on it. The law even went into specific detail about what the provider was supposed to describe to the patient.

The law had other provisions deemed highly objectionable by reproductive rights advocates, including a requirement that providers transmit extensive (and, some say, irrelevant and highly personal) information about patients to a state agency.

Ultrasound requirements are the latest strategy on a growing list of tactics that reproductive rights foes have turned to in recent years to further their aim of curtailing access to abortion. According to Guttmacher data, 17 states have mandated counseling provisions, including some that some medical authorities say exaggerate or misstate the risks of the procedure; 24 states have mandatory waiting periods, usually 24 hours, that can force a woman to take two separate trips to obtain the procedure; and 35 states have some parental involvement requirement.

The Effect of Restrictions on the Abortion Rate

So are these measures bringing down abortion rates? Data show abortions have declined in recent years in the U.S., but experts say multiple factors are responsible.

One recent report showed U.S. abortion rates have declined from a high of about 30 per 1,000 women in 1980 to about 20 per 1,000 women in 2005.

Researchers believe that the main factors bringing down abortion rates are improvements in the access to and use of contraception, and sexuality education programs. Some evidence shows abortion restrictions may have had a small but insignificant effect on reducing surgical abortions, but they also are fueling other trends.

FAST FACT

According to the Guttmacher Institute, the US abortion rate in 2008 was 19.6 women per 1,000 overall, but among poor women it was 52.2 per 1,000.

Such restrictions undoubtedly are one reason use of RU 486, the so-called abortion pill, has skyrocketed in recent years. One report showed that the drug accounted for 13 percent of all abortions in 2005, an increase from 6 percent in 2001. Nearly a quarter of early abortions were performed with RU 486. What's more, doctors other than ob/gyns [obstetricians/gynecologists] are now prescribing RU 486, making it more widely available.

An analysis by Rachel Benston Gold for the Guttmacher Institute, published earlier this year [2009], concluded that measures aimed at dissuading women from having abortions "do not appear to be effective in . . . materially reducing the number of procedures performed."

She cited a review of studies by Guttmacher, Ibis Reproductive Health and Baruch College which found that such measures "by and large . . . do not prevent abortions." This review called the strategy "largely unsuccessful."

Harms to Disadvantaged Women and Minors

One "clear exception," they concluded, was disadvantaged women, who "often don't have the resources to navigate the hurdles" imposed by such restrictions.

Parental involvement laws "do little to affect the abortion rate," this trio concluded, with one possible exception: Such laws may have contributed to an increase in the teen birth rate in Texas where teens were not able to travel the distances required to access out-of-state services.

Waiting periods, similarly, have kept some disadvantaged women from accessing abortion because the two-visit requirement has proven

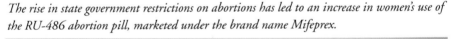

The rise in state government restrictions on abortions has led to an increase in women's use of the RU-486 abortion pill, marketed under the brand name Mifeprex.

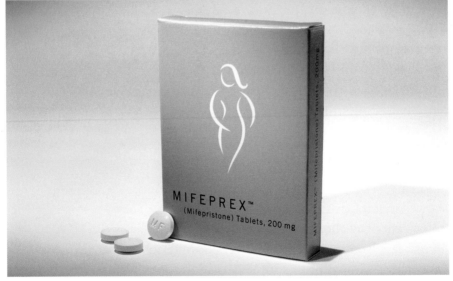

insurmountable to some, but have not been much of a problem for higher-income women.

Pointing to data showing that "almost all women obtaining abortions are sure of their decision . . . before they have even picked up the phone to make an appointment," Gold argues it's not likely women will be swayed by "inaccurate and emotionally laden attempts to persuade them otherwise."

It's instructive to look at the experience of other countries that have turned to tough restrictions in hopes of reducing abortion. In Africa, Latin America and the Caribbean, where abortion laws are among the most restrictive, the regional rates are between 29 and 31 per 1,000 women. Brazil, Chile and Peru, which also have severe restrictions, have abortion rates between 40 and 55 per 1,000 women.

European countries, where restrictions are scant, have the lowest abortion rates: around 10 per 1,000 women or less.

It should be axiomatic that preventing unwanted pregnancies in the first place should be the first and foremost priority. But for some reason, there's a strong tendency in this country to punish women in crisis and make them suffer more. Why on Earth would that be?

EVALUATING THE AUTHOR'S ARGUMENTS:

In this viewpoint Janet Pearson suggests that the abortion rates of a given country are tied to the level of restrictions the country has on abortion. What other explanation might account for the difference in abortion rates among countries?

Viewpoint

5

Abortion Should Be Completely Restricted Without Exceptions

Leslie Tignor

"Abortion always claims a human person's life, and therefore is never an appropriate choice."

In the following viewpoint Leslie Tignor argues that there is never a justification for allowing abortion and, thus, abortion should be restricted without exception. Tignor considers three situations often used to justify abortion and rejects each. She claims that it is not reasonable to murder an innocent child created by rape or incest. She also denies that fetal deformity justifies abortion. Finally, she argues that abortion is not justified when a woman's life is at stake, claiming that the woman may receive medical treatment to save her life that may or may not result in the death of her fetus. Tignor is director of the associate program at the American Life League, an antiabortion organization.

Leslie Tignor, "Abortion 'Exceptions,'" American Life League, February 23, 2010. www.all.org. Copyright © 2010 by American Life League, Inc. All rights reserved. Reproduced by permission.

AS YOU READ, CONSIDER THE FOLLOWING QUESTIONS:
  1. The author contends that abortion in the case of rape or incest does not solve a victim's problem but, rather, does what?
  2. What two examples of killing does Tignor use to back up her claim that aborting a disabled person in the womb is unjustified?
  3. Medical treatment that results in the death of a fetus is justified by what principle, according to Tignor?

The idea of a total ban on all abortions makes some people uncomfortable. After all, we've been told for years that there are situations in which abortion, though a poor choice, is the best option. That, however, is untrue. Abortion always claims a human person's life, and therefore is never an appropriate choice.

The "big lie" theory says [that] if an untrue statement is repeated often enough, the people will start to accept it as truth. Such is the case with the erroneous mantra that abortion must be permitted in cases of rape, incest, fetal deformity and threat to the mother's life.

Abortion in Cases of Rape and Incest

Rape and incest are similar in the sense that both are criminal acts. In our system of justice, we punish the criminal. We do not punish the victim, nor do we punish the criminal's children. We are told, however, that if pregnancy occurs as a result of rape or incest, offering the victim an abortion is the compassionate thing to do. No woman should be "forced to carry that monster's child," we are told.

The trauma of sexual assault is very real, and there is no intention here to downplay that. Abortion carries its own variety of trauma, however; women—even those who were victims of sexual assault—have reported years of physical, emotional and psychological difficulty following their abortions. Abortion did not solve their problem; it merely created additional ones.

There is also the very important fact that abortion takes the life of a living human being. The circumstances of conception may have been criminal, but the life of the newly-created human being is just as valuable as any other person's. We do not put criminals' innocent

Kansas legislators hold a press conference to announce the introduction of a bill calling for stricter enforcement of the state's late-term abortion law.

children to death in our culture; it simply isn't done. It should not be done in this situation, either.

Abortion for Fetal Abnormality

Expectant parents can treat a diagnosis of fetal deformity or other form of birth defect almost as if it were death itself. It is not a physical death, but a death of hopes and dreams. Visions of a "normal" childhood—playing games, going to school, growing up and starting families of their own—vanish in a flash. Parents in this moment of despair are often told they should simply go ahead and terminate the pregnancy and get on with their lives.

The first problem here is that medical opinions can be just that—opinions. There are countless cases of parents who permitted their children to live and found out at birth that the experts were wrong. Also, imagine the horror of the parents who abort their child, only to see that they had destroyed a perfect baby. That is simply too difficult to comprehend.

Abortions in case of fetal abnormality, however, are just like all other abortions. They take the lives of innocent human beings. Abortions in these cases raise frightening prospects, for if it is all right to kill a disabled person in the womb, could it one day be considered permissible to kill a disabled infant? A disabled adult? The answer is clearly "no" in those cases; why is there any question when the victim is a child in the womb?

Abortion to Save the Mother's Life

This excuse for allowing abortion sounds reasonable. If the pregnancy is threatening the mother's life, it would seem that lethal force—an abortion—would be a permissible form of self-defense. The child is not really "attacking" the mother, but his presence puts her at risk. It sounds like a good argument, but it simply isn't true.

Hundreds of doctors have signed a statement that puts the situation in perspective. The statement reads, "There is never a situation in the law or in the ethical practice of medicine where a preborn child's life need be intentionally destroyed by procured abortion for the purpose of saving the life of the mother. A physician must do everything possible to save the lives of both of his patients, mother and child. He must never intend the death of either."

A tubal (or ectopic) pregnancy, for instance, can indeed be life-threatening. But the treatment, even if it is fatal to the child, is not a

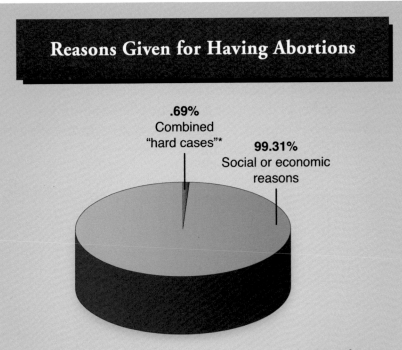

Reasons Given for Having Abortions

.69%
Combined
"hard cases"*

99.31%
Social or economic
reasons

*Hard cases include abortion to save the woman's life—in cases of rape or incest—and for fetal deformity.

Taken from: Human Life International, "Exception: Is Abortion Even Permissible?," *Pro-Life Talking Points*, 2010.

"procured abortion." The doctor wants to save the baby, but knows that is unlikely. The baby's death is an unintended consequence of the physician's effort to save the mother. There are similar cases involving the treatment of cancer in which the baby's death can be an unintended consequence. But again, these are medical treatments, not abortion.

It is important to distinguish between direct abortion, which is the intentional and willed destruction of a preborn child, and a legitimate treatment a pregnant mother may choose to save her life. Operations that are performed to save the life of the mother—such as the removal of a cancerous uterus or an ectopic pregnancy that poses the threat of imminent death—are considered indirect abortions.

They are justified under a concept called the "principle of double effect." Under this principle, the death of the child is an unintended effect of an operation independently justified by the necessity of saving the mother's life.

Essentially, both mother and child should be treated as patients. A doctor should try to protect both. However, in the course of treating a woman, if her child dies, that is not considered abortion.

There is only one purpose for abortion—ending the life of the child. The "life of the mother" situation for abortion is simply bogus.

EVALUATING THE AUTHOR'S ARGUMENTS:

In this viewpoint Leslie Tignor argues that abortion is not even justified in the hardest of cases. Name at least two other viewpoints in this volume that reflect this view.

Parental Involvement Laws Should Be Required for a Minor's Abortion

Maggie Datiles

"In order to protect the health and safety of minors and the constitutional rights of parents . . . it is essential for the states to enact parental involvement laws."

In the following viewpoint Maggie Datiles argues that parental notification laws and parental consent laws are needed to protect minors and to protect the rights of parents. Datiles contends that parental involvement laws help protect the health and safety of minors by allowing parents to offer medical information and provide for necessary care after an abortion. She also argues that parents have a right to know about their daughter's abortion, pointing to a long history by the US Supreme Court of recognizing the rights of parents to have authority over their children. Datiles is an associate fellow in law at the Culture of Life Foundation and staff attorney for Americans United for Life, both pro-life organizations.

AS YOU READ, CONSIDER THE FOLLOWING QUESTIONS:
1. According to Datiles, what do parental notification laws typically require?
2. Datiles claims that parental involvement statutes protect the health of minors by providing parents with the opportunity to do what?
3. What two quotes by the US Supreme Court does the author give in support of parental rights?

A ccompanying the increasing cultural acceptance of abortion is a proportionate increase in the necessity for parental involvement laws. The promotion of sex-with-no-consequences in America has generated a high demand for abortion, including abortions for minors. These abortions present a host of issues not present in adult abortions: (1) the state's interest in protecting the health and welfare of minors; (2) the state's interest in protecting the constitutional rights of parents to raise their children; (3) immature minors' lack of ability to make fully-informed decisions that take into account both immediate and long-range medical, emotional, and psychological consequences of abortion; and (4) ensuring care that takes into account her medical history.

In light of the differences between minor and adult abortions, how important are parental involvement laws? How have the courts and legislatures treated parental involvement laws? And in the absence of parental involvement laws, what is at stake for minors and parents?

Parental Notification and Consent Laws

The two forms of parental involvement laws for abortion are parental notification laws and parental consent laws. Parental notification laws typically require abortion providers to give 48 hours notice of a minor or incompetent person's abortion to a parent or legal guardian. Parental consent laws, on the other hand, require abortion providers to secure the actual consent of a parent or legal guardian before performing an abortion.

The United States Supreme Court (USSC) has consistently held that both parental notification and consent laws are constitutional and do not impose an undue burden on a woman's right to abortion when such laws contain (1) an exception for medical emergencies or when notice is waived by the person entitled to such notice; and (2) a confidential judicial bypass procedure. A judicial bypass is, in essence, the substitution of the court's permission for the abortion for the requisite parental or guardian involvement. Such bypasses are generally granted when a court finds that a minor is mature and well-informed enough to make the abortion decision, or when a court finds that the minor has been subject to physical, sexual, or emotional abuse by the parent or guardian. For example, a judicial bypass may be granted if a court finds that the pregnancy is a result of incest by the parent who is to receive notice, or if the minor is in danger of physical abuse by the parent who is to be notified. Moreover, some states even have specific exceptions within the statute itself for cases of incest and physical abuse.

Arkansas governor Mike Huckabee signs a 2005 bill requiring parental notification for a minor's abortion. Many states have passed similar laws.

The most common argument against parental involvement laws is that parental involvement laws could put certain minors in danger of abuse by their parent(s) or guardian(s), and would force such minors to seek out illegal abortions. The exception to the parental involvements laws for cases of sexual, physical and emotional abuse clearly anticipates and rebuts this argument.

Further argument against parental involvement laws are that such laws assume that all minors are immature and unable to make decisions in their own best interests, and that parental involvement laws will be unnecessarily applied to mature minors who are capable of making their own. These arguments are easily countered by the existence of confidential judicial bypass provisions which allow a court to authorize a minor's abortion without parental notice and/or consent upon a finding that a minor is mature and able to make a fully-informed decision that takes into consideration the physical, mental and emotional consequences of abortion.

The Need to Protect Minors

Parental involvement laws are clearly necessary for the health, safety and welfare of minors. Indeed, on several occasions, the USSC has recognized that minors seeking abortions presents a unique set of concerns that are not present with adults and that special legal protections are necessary to address these concerns.

One issue specifically implicated is access to the minor's medical records and other important health information. Parental involvement statutes provide parents the opportunity to supply the abortion provider with the minor's medical and health information, as well as an opportunity for the parents to discuss and arrange adequate post-abortion care. Without these opportunities for parent-physician consultation and cooperation, the health of minors is put at serious risk. An abortion provider should know the medical history and background of the woman seeking an abortion, to make the best medical judgment regarding whether or not an abortion would be in the best interests of the woman, as well as any special health needs or accommodations the woman will need prior to, during, and after the abortion.

Parental involvement laws guarantee that parents will be available to help their daughters in cases of medical emergencies arising from an abortion. In February 1994, 15-year-old "Sarah" had an abortion at the hands of Moshe Hachamovitch at "A to Z Women's Services" in Houston, Texas, without her parents' notice or consent. Hachamovitch tore the right side of her cervix during the abortion. For four days, Sarah suffered at home from blood poisoning, fever, chills, severe abdominal pain, and nausea. She was completely unaware of the tear in her cervix, and her parents had no idea that she had had an abortion. She died in a hospital intensive care unit on March 2, 1992. The hospital physicians reported that if Sarah had received prompt medical care, the tear and post-abortion infection would have been detected immediately, and she would not have died. Had Sarah's parents been aware of her abortion and given the opportunity to arrange adequate post-abortion care, Sarah would still be alive today.

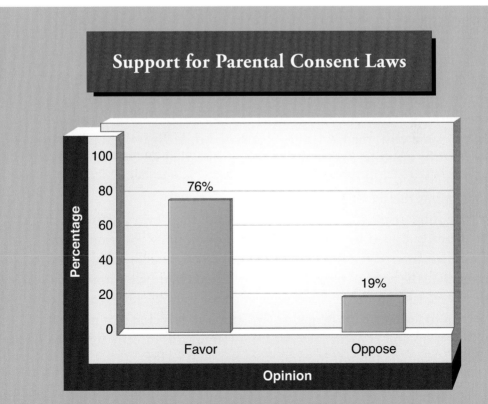

Support for Parental Consent Laws

Taken from: Pew Forum on Religion & Public Life, "2009 Annual Religion and Public Life Survey, 2009."

Thus, it is clear that parental involvement laws directly serve the state's legitimate interest in protecting the health and safety of minors.

Parental involvement laws are also necessary for truly informed consent to be obtained. Parental advice and emotional support is irreplaceable for a minor's abortion decision. The USSC has emphasized that "[a]s immature minors often lack the ability to make fully informed choices that take account of both immediate and long-range consequences, a State reasonably may determine that parental consultation often is desirable and in the best interest of the minor." Indeed, the Court has recognized that the state's legitimate interest in ensuring that a minor's abortion decision is informed justifies the enactment of parental involvement laws, as the abortion decision "is a grave decision, and a girl of tender years, under emotional stress, may be ill-equipped to make it without mature advice and emotional support."

The Protection of Parental Rights

Lastly, parental involvement laws are necessary for the protection of parental rights. Parents have a right to know if their minor child will be undergoing an abortion, an invasive and often dangerous surgical procedure. The constitutional and traditional right of parents to rear their children has long been acknowledged by the courts. The USSC states that "constitutional interpretation has consistently recognized that the parents' claim to authority in their own household to direct the rearing of their children is basic in the structure of our society." In the same vein, the Court has also stated that: "It is cardinal with us that the custody, care and nurture of the child reside first in the parents, whose primary function and freedom include preparation for obligations the state can neither supply nor hinder."

The fundamental right of parents to raise their own children can be directly applied in the context of minors seeking abortions. The Court has interpreted the right of parents to raise their own children to include the right of parents to counsel their children on important decisions, such as the decision as to whether to carry a pregnancy to term or to terminate the pregnancy by abortion. It is clear that parental notification and consent laws for minor abortions directly serve the state's legitimate interest in protecting parental rights. . . .

In order to protect the health and safety of minors and the constitutional rights of parents to rear their children, it is essential for the states to enact parental involvement laws. The USSC has made it abundantly clear that such laws are constitutional when drafted properly and further important legitimate state interests. The safety of minors and the rights of parents demand no less.

EVALUATING THE AUTHOR'S ARGUMENTS:

In this viewpoint Maggie Datiles contends that parental notification laws and parental consent laws are necessary to protect the health and safety of minors. What does NARAL Pro-Choice America, author of the following viewpoint, argue that directly contradicts this view?

Parental Involvement Laws Should Not Be Required for a Minor's Abortion

NARAL Pro-Choice America Foundation

"Mandatory parental-involvement (consent and notice) laws . . . only exacerbate a potentially dangerous situation."

In the following viewpoint the NARAL Pro-Choice America Foundation argues that parental involvement laws—requiring either parental notice or parental consent—are not a good idea. Though enacted with the goal of increasing parental involvement, NARAL argues that parental involvement laws fail to take into account the reality of many family situations that are not helped by laws mandating communication. Furthermore, NARAL claims that rather than making minors safer, parental involvement laws actually often put young pregnant women in danger. NARAL Pro-Choice America is an advocacy group that works to protect a woman's right to choose.

AS YOU READ, CONSIDER THE FOLLOWING QUESTIONS:
1. According to the author, what two pieces of federal legislation have been proposed to further parental involvement in abortion?
2. NARAL Pro-Choice America claims that what percentage of minors who did not tell a parent about their abortion had experienced violence or feared violence?
3. What does the author think is an inadequate alternative to parental involvement?

There are two types of parental-involvement laws; those that require parental *notice* and those that require parental *consent* before a minor can seek abortion services. Parental-notice laws require prior written notification of parents before an abortion can be performed, with limited exceptions, such as in cases of physical abuse, incest, or medical emergency. These laws also may prescribe other preconditions including a mandatory waiting period following the parents' receipt of notification, and/or judicial intervention if there are compelling reasons to avoid parental notification.

Parental-consent laws require that minors obtain the consent of one or both parents before they can receive abortion services. As is the case with parental notice, a judicial-bypass process is also included in parental-consent laws. The penalties for violating parental-consent laws range from civil liability and fines to imprisonment. The Supreme Court has ruled that parental-consent requirements are constitutional so long as they include a judicial-bypass procedure to accommodate those young women who cannot involve their parents.

> **FAST FACT**
>
> California, Montana, Nevada, New Jersey, and New Mexico all enacted parental involvement laws that have been found to be unconstitutional and unenforceable.

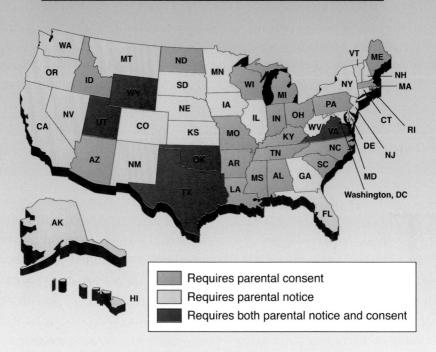

States That Enforce Parental Involvement Laws for Abortion

Requires parental consent

Requires parental notice

Requires both parental notice and consent

Taken from: NARAL Pro-Choice America, "Restrictions on Young Women's Access to Abortion," 2011. www.prochoiceamerica.org/what-is-choice/fast-facts/young-women.html.

Parental Involvement Through Legislation

Ideally, a teen facing a crisis will seek the advice and counsel of those who care for her most and know her best. In fact, even in the absence of laws mandating parental involvement, many young women do turn to their parents when they are considering abortion. Unfortunately, some young women cannot involve their parents because physical violence or emotional abuse is present in their homes, because their pregnancies are the result of incest, or because they fear parental anger and disappointment. Mandatory parental-involvement (consent and notice) laws do not solve the problem of inadequate family communication; they only exacerbate a potentially dangerous situation.

In some circumstances, teens facing an unintended pregnancy feel compelled to travel to another state where there is a less stringent parental-involvement law or no such law at all to avoid involving their parents and maintain their privacy. In the most dire of circumstances, some pregnant young women who fear telling their parents may resort to illegal or self-induced abortions that may result in death. Yet, despite these severe consequences, 38 states currently enforce laws that require a minor to obtain the consent of, or notify, an adult—typically a parent —prior to an abortion. And five other states have minors' access laws that are either enjoined or not enforced.

In recent years, anti-choice legislators in Congress have attempted to pass two pieces of federal legislation that would impose draconian criminal parental-involvement laws on every state in the country. The first, called the "Child Custody Protection Act [CCPA]," criminalizes caring and loving adults—including grandparents, adult siblings, and religious counselors—who accompany a teen out of state for abortion care if the home state parental-involvement law has not been met. The second, called the "Child Interstate Abortion Notification Act," in addition to the restrictive provisions in the CCPA, also would impose a convoluted patchwork of parental-involvement laws on women and doctors across the country, making it virtually impossible for young women to access abortion services in another state. Both measures would threaten young women's health and deny them the support and guidance they need from responsible and caring adults.

The Issue of Family Dynamics

Government cannot mandate healthy family communication. Laws requiring parental notice or consent actually may endanger the young women they purport to protect by increasing the possibility of illegal and self-induced abortion, family violence, suicide, later abortions, and unwanted childbirth.

- A majority of young adults who are pregnant and seek abortion care indicate that their parents are aware that they are doing so. Furthermore, in states without parental-involvement laws, 61 percent of parents knew of their daughter's decision to terminate a pregnancy. . . .

Most young women find love, support, and safety in their home. Many, however, justifiably fear that they would be physically or emotionally abused if forced to disclose their pregnancy. Often, young women who do not involve a parent come from families where government-mandated disclosure would have devastating effects.

- An estimated 772,000 children were found to be victims of abuse or neglect in 2008. Young women considering abortion are particularly vulnerable because research shows that family violence is often at its worst during a family member's pregnancy.
- Nearly half of pregnant teens who have a history of abuse report being assaulted during their pregnancy, most often by a family member. As the Supreme Court has recognized, "Mere notification of pregnancy is frequently a flashpoint for battering and violence within the family. The number of battering incidents is high during the pregnancy and often the worst abuse can be associated with pregnancy."
- Among minors who did not tell a parent of their abortion, 30 percent had experienced violence in their family or feared violence or being forced to leave home. "My older sister got pregnant when she was seventeen. My mother pushed her against the wall, slapped her across the face and then grabbed her by the hair, pulled her through the living room out the front door and threw her off the porch. We don't know where she is now."
- In Idaho, a 13-year-old student named Spring Adams was shot to death by her father after he learned she was to terminate a pregnancy caused by his acts of incest.

The Risk of Danger to Young Women
Parental-consent and notice laws endanger young women's health by forcing some women—even some from healthy, loving families—to turn to illegal or self-induced abortion, delay the procedure and increase the medical risk, or bear a child against their will.

- In Indiana, Rebecca Bell, a young woman who had a very close relationship with her parents, died from an illegal abortion that she sought because she did not want her parents to know about her pregnancy. Indiana law required parental consent before she could have a legal abortion. . . .

In challenges to two different parental-involvement laws, the Supreme Court has ruled that a state statute requiring parental involvement must have some sort of bypass procedure, such as a judicial bypass, in order to be constitutional. And that no one person may have an absolute veto over a minor's decision to have an abortion. Thus, most states that require parental consent or notice provide—at least as a matter of law—a judicial

Nancy Keenan, president of the National Abortion Rights Action League (NARAL), speaks at an event marking the anniversary of Roe v. Wade. *NARAL has been at the forefront in the fight against laws restricting abortion.*

bypass through which a young woman can seek a court order allowing an abortion without parental involvement.

But bypass procedures are often an inadequate alternative for young women, especially when courts are either not equipped or resistant to granting judicial bypasses. Even for adults, going to court for a judicial order is difficult. For young women without a lawyer, it is overwhelming and at times impossible. Some young women cannot maneuver the legal procedures required or cannot attend hearings scheduled during school hours. Others do not go or delay going because they fear that the proceedings are not confidential or that they will be recognized by people at the courthouse. Many experience fear and distress and do not want to reveal intimate details of their personal lives to strangers. Time required to schedule the court proceeding may result in a delay of a week or more, thereby increasing the health risks of the abortion. And in many instances, courts are not equipped to handle bypass proceedings in accord with constitutional regulations. Worse yet, some young women who do manage to arrange a hearing face judges who are vehemently anti-choice and who routinely deny petitions of minors who show that they are mature or that the bypass is in their best interest, despite rulings by the U.S. Supreme Court that the bypass must be granted in those circumstances.

EVALUATING THE AUTHOR'S ARGUMENTS:

In this viewpoint the NARAL Pro-Choice America Foundation argues against parental involvement laws because of their negative impacts on young women. Reflecting on the previous viewpoint by Maggie Datiles, how do you think NARAL would respond to the issue of parental rights?

Does Legal Abortion Benefit or Harm Society?

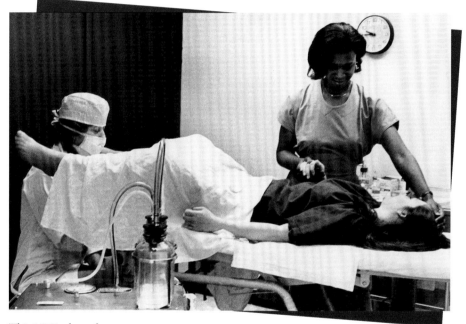

This 1978 photo shows a woman undergoing an abortion at a New York City abortion clinic.

Roe v. Wade Has Advanced Women's Equality

"At the core of women's equality is the ability to control whether and when we have children."

Deborah Jacobs

In the following viewpoint Deborah Jacobs contends that great strides have been made in the equality of women since the US Supreme Court's decision protecting a woman's right to abortion in *Roe v. Wade* in 1973. Jacobs claims that since 1973, women's advances are evident by the increase in the number of women in politics. Additionally, Jacobs notes that women now attend college in greater numbers and are represented more in business. She warns that in the debate over abortion, the equality gains of women should not be forgotten. Jacobs is executive director of the American Civil Liberties Union of New Jersey.

AS YOU READ, CONSIDER THE FOLLOWING QUESTIONS:
1. According to Jacobs, in 1973 how many women had ever served as a state governor?
2. By what factor did the number of female CEOs grow from 1973 to 2006, according to the author?
3. Jacobs contends that what connection has been lost in the political fighting over abortion?

C ome election day, abortion will likely be on voters' minds as candidates pull out the abortion card to cast aspersions on their opponents or stake claim to a constituency. Some voters will vote for or against candidates because of their position on the issue. Few, however, will consider what is really at stake in the abortion question: women's equality.

Political Gains by Women

Roe v. Wade turns 35 today [January 22, 2008]. With this anniversary we mark not only 35 years of reproductive freedom, but 35 years of impressive gains in the fight for women's equality.

Granted, these were not perfect years. Not all women have had equal access to reproductive health care: Poor women, teens and women living in rural communities have increasingly faced real obstacles because of government restrictions. Likewise, not all women have benefited equally in the expansion of women's access to higher education, better paying jobs or other socioeconomic gains.

And as with the fight for reproductive freedom, the struggle for women's equality is far from over.

Nevertheless, these decades have witnessed important advances for many women. The numbers alone tell a significant piece of the story: Thirty-five years ago, there were

FAST FACT

In 2009 Sonia Sotomayor became the third woman to serve on the US Supreme Court, replacing retired justice David Souter.

15 women in Congress. Today, 92 women sit in Congress, including the first Madame Speaker.

In 1973, the number of women who had ever been governor totaled three. As of today [January 22, 2008], 26 women have served as governor.

And in the race for president, for the first time in our nation's history, a woman [Hillary Rodham Clinton] is one of the leading contenders for the nomination of a major political party. . . .

A Growth in Equality

The political arena has not been alone in this transformation. Women make up 57 percent of college students (up from 42 percent in 1970)

and are obtaining advanced degrees in record numbers. In the mid-Seventies, women made up only 16 percent of medical school graduates; today they constitute nearly 50 percent. Likewise, women holding science and engineering doctoral degrees have more than quadrupled since the late Sixties.

The ranks of female Fortune 500 CEOs [chief executive officers] have grown from one in 1973 to 10 in 2006.

The timing of these advances is not serendipitous. At the core of women's equality is the ability to control whether and when we have children. The legalization of contraception in the Sixties and abortion in the Seventies fostered women's ability to make important life decisions about themselves and their families.

This fact is not lost on the only two women ever to serve on the Supreme Court. Justice Sandra Day O'Connor co-authored an opinion preserving *Roe* in 1992 that acknowledged, "The ability of women to participate equally in the economic and social life of the

US senators gather on Capitol Hill. When Roe v. Wade *was decided in 1973, there were only fifteen women in Congress; today there are ninety-two.*

Percent of All College Degrees Female Versus Male, 1949–2010

○ Male
● Female

Taken from: Mark J. Perry, "The Gender Degree Gap and the Great Mancession," MrSwing.com, March 17, 2010/ US Department of Education.

nation has been facilitated by their ability to control their reproductive lives."

And just last year [2007], in a powerful dissent to a Supreme Court decision upholding the first-ever federal ban on certain abortion procedures, Justice Ruth Bader Ginsburg passionately argued that the core of the right to abortion "center[s] on a woman's autonomy to determine her life's course, and thus to enjoy equal citizenship stature."

Reproductive Rights and Equality

Yet, as we mark the 35th anniversary of *Roe v. Wade*, the connection between reproductive rights and gender equality is lost in the political wrangling over abortion.

It is time to step back and reexamine the role access to birth control and abortion plays not only in opening up the classrooms, boardrooms and legislatures to women, but to ensuring women's equality more broadly.

It is time to refocus the conversation on fairness and opportunity so that we all can make meaningful decisions about whether and when to bear children.

The political, economic and social life of our democracy depends on it.

> **EVALUATING THE AUTHOR'S ARGUMENTS:**
>
> In this viewpoint Deborah Jacobs contends that the constitutional protection of a woman's right to abortion has increased women's equality. What response might Janice Shaw Crouse, author of the following viewpoint, have to this claim?

Viewpoint 2

Roe v. Wade Has Not Resulted in Progress

Janice Shaw Crouse

"When we look at the birthrate in the United States beginning in 1900, we see a very different picture than the progress-began-with-Roe-v-Wade folks imply."

In the following viewpoint Janice Shaw Crouse contends that the claim that progress for women resulted from the US Supreme Court's decision protecting a woman's right to abortion in *Roe v. Wade* (1973) is false. She argues that the facts do not back up this claim. Crouse says that although after *Roe* the overall birthrate dropped, she claims it has resulted in a far greater birthrate among unwed women. Thus, she contends there is no reason to believe that legal abortion has resulted in progress by reducing the number of unwanted children. Crouse is a senior fellow at the Beverly LaHaye Institute, the think tank for Concerned Women for America. She is author of *Children at Risk: The Precarious State of Children's Well-Being in America*.

AS YOU READ, CONSIDER THE FOLLOWING QUESTIONS:
  1. According to Crouse, what piece of legislation regarding abortion overseas angered the political Left?
  2. The author states that compared with 1933, the birthrate has declined by what percentage?
  3. Crouse claims that the birthrate of unmarried women increased by 93 percent in what time period?

I n a speech delivered in Atlanta over the weekend [October 21, 2007], Supreme Court Justice Ruth Bader Ginsburg declared that banning abortion "would have a devastating impact on poor women." Bader's suggestion, that abortion is a solution to the problems of poor women, is on a par with Jonathan Swift's long-ago solution to the Irish poverty problem in his essay, *A Modest Proposal* [suggesting that the Irish eat their children]. At least Swift was writing satire.

The Importance of Facts

"Facts," as [American founding father] John Adams stated so clearly, "are stubborn things; and whatever may be our wishes, our inclinations, or the dictates of our passion, they cannot alter the state of facts and evidence." Yet, conservative critiques of leftist [liberal] policy proposals, no matter how carefully buttressed by facts, are swept aside lightly and dismissed as irrelevant by media, historians and biographers. Many distorted views go unchallenged in the public arena simply because so few have looked (or are willing to look) at the facts.

Worse still, when the actual facts don't agree with the Left's latest political nostrum, they are drowned out by the claim that those "old" facts have been superseded by the results of some new study that purports to show that "up" is now "down." Nowhere is this encountered more frequently than in the Left's assaults on any and all boundaries relating to sex, marriage, family and child rearing.

For example, the Left is furious with [President] George [W.] Bush for (among other things) reinstating the "Mexico City Policy," first instituted by [President] Ronald Reagan [and rescinded by President

Barack Obama in 2009], that makes the receipt of federal funds by non-governmental organizations conditional upon their agreeing that they will "neither perform nor actively promote abortion as a method of family planning in other nations." It is bizarre how the Left can howl about how inhumane it is to use the interrogation technique of "waterboarding" (which does no lasting physical harm) to extract information from terrorists, but they are just fine and dandy with death by dismemberment of unborn babies in the womb.

FAST FACT

In 2010, three years after the recession began, the National Center for Health Statistics reported that the birthrate had dropped to its lowest level in at least a century.

To read their pious-sounding rhetoric about how essential the barbaric practice of abortion is to the health and well-being of women, one would be forgiven for thinking that abortion was the cornerstone of progress, that civilization only began to make headway when abortion became legal in this country. And naturally, feminists just want to share this priceless, newly-minted benefit with all the oppressed women of the world, who presumably have no other means of avoiding the Malthusian[1] spectre: unending pregnancies and starving mouths to feed.

The Birth Rate in the United States

But what are the actual facts of the matter?

When we look at the birthrate in the United States beginning in 1900, we see a very different picture than the progress-began-with-*Roe-v-Wade* folks imply. From 1900 to 1933, the birthrate declined 44 percent *without the pill* and *without legal abortion.* The post–WWII baby boom of the 1950s aside, the birthrate today is only 15 percent lower than it was in 1933.

Does abortion then actually lower the birthrate? To test this idea, it would seem that if this were the case, the effect would show up most

---

1. Eighteenth-century English thinker Thomas Malthus warned that global overpopulation would one day put an end to human progress.

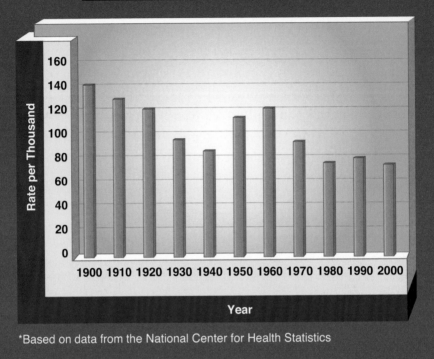

Birth Rate for US Women Aged Fifteen to Forty-Four*

*Based on data from the National Center for Health Statistics

Taken from: Janice Shaw Crouse, "Did Progress Begin with *Roe v. Wade*?," Concerned Women for America, October 26, 2007.

powerfully in the birthrate of unmarried women, who presumably would be most inclined to resort to abortion to escape the responsibilities of an unplanned, unwanted pregnancy. Here again, the facts run against the conclusion that the Left would have us assume—without proof—to be the case.

The "legalization" of abortion initially produced only a very modest decrease in the unwed birthrate. Subsequently, the increase in non-marital, promiscuous sexual activity—promoted by the same folks who championed abortion as the panacea for unwanted births—produced a 93 percent increase in the birthrate of unmarried women from 1973 to 1994. The unwed birthrate in 2004 was the same as it was in 1994, despite the fact that the unwed abortion rate has been declining. (The abortion rate among unmarried women peaked in 1981 and has declined by 37 percent.)

A Lens of Self-Absorption

It can be difficult to rid young children of the conceit that they are the center of the universe and that the only things of any importance are those that focus on them. This creates the propensity to look at life primarily through the lens of what they know from their own limited experience. Likewise, feminists from the Western World see through a gaze clouded by self-absorption. They are blind to the [testimony] of history. They care nothing about how the birthrate changed before and after the legalization of abortion. They will allow nothing to sway them, to deter them from their tireless efforts through the U.N. to export to the third world the plague of death which has brought "demographic winter" to Europe.

Janice Shaw Crouse (pictured) of the Beverly LaHaye Institute, a conservative think tank, authored this viewpoint. She argues that because of Roe v. Wade, *unwed American women are far more likely to have children.*

The fact is, we could and should be doing more to help poor nations around the world by providing technology and resources for the things that are essential to life and health, things like clean, unpolluted drinking water. Funding abortion in third world countries, however, is another matter altogether. No amount of language twisting—calling it "family planning" or "women's reproductive health care"—will mask the true horror of abortion. The Scripture teaches us, "There is a way which seems right to a man, but its end is the way of death" (Proverbs 14:12).

EVALUATING THE AUTHOR'S ARGUMENTS:

In this viewpoint Janice Shaw Crouse contends that the rise in the birthrate among unwed women since *Roe v. Wade* (1973) is not a sign of progress. How might an opponent argue that it is a sign of progress?

Legal Abortion Saves Women's Lives

"In the years since Roe v. Wade was decided, thousands of American women's lives have been saved by access to legal abortion."

NARAL Pro-Choice America Foundation

In the following viewpoint NARAL Pro-Choice America argues that the constitutional protection of a woman's right to abortion in *Roe v. Wade* (1973) has led to gains in women's health and the avoidance of unnecessary deaths from illegal abortions. NARAL claims that attacks on a woman's right to choose by government regulations and restrictions currently makes it difficult for women to access safe abortion. The author argues that early abortion is extremely safe and that without legal abortion, complications to women's health and increased mortality would result from illegal abortions. NARAL Pro-Choice America is an advocacy group that works to protect a woman's right to choose.

AS YOU READ, CONSIDER THE FOLLOWING QUESTIONS:
1. NARAL Pro-Choice America claims that antichoice groups are trying to restrict access to what abortion drug?
2. According to the author, what percentage of abortions take place in the first twelve weeks of pregnancy?
3. How many women worldwide obtain abortions illegally each year, as reported in the viewpoint?

As part of their strategy to make abortion illegal and unavailable, anti-choice forces make unsubstantiated claims that *legal* abortion is harmful to women's health. The fact is that the decriminalization of abortion in the United States in 1973 has led to tremendous gains in protecting women's health. The Institute of Medicine of the National Academy of Sciences declared in its first major study of abortion in 1975 that "legislation and practices that permit women to obtain abortions in proper medical surroundings will lead to fewer deaths and a lower rate of medical complications than [will] restrictive legislation and practices." The American Medical Association's Council on Scientific Affairs reaffirmed this finding in 1992 when it attributed the marked decline in deaths from abortion services to "the shift from illegal to legal abortion," along with the introduction of antibiotics and the widespread use of effective contraception in the 1960s. Furthermore, the experience in the United States is very similar to that in Western Europe, where mortality rates from abortion services were reduced after legal abortion became widely available.

The Safety of Legal Abortion

In the years since *Roe v. Wade* was decided, thousands of American women's lives have been saved by access to legal abortion care. Nonetheless, *Roe* and the availability of legal abortion services, as well as the progress women have achieved for reproductive freedom, are under constant attack. Mandatory waiting periods, biased counseling requirements, restrictions on young women's access, costly and unnecessary regulations, and limited public funding have had a cumulative impact, making it increasingly difficult for women to obtain safe abortion care. Aggravating the problem, the number of abortion providers continues to decline; anti-choice forces have created an atmosphere of intense intimidation and violence that deters physicians from entering the field and has caused others to stop providing abortion services. The most recent, tragic example was the 2009 murder of Dr. George Tiller, an abortion provider, in Wichita, Kansas. Ironically, many of those now raising alarms about the supposed dangers of abortion are the very people whose public policy suggestions would make exercising reproductive rights more hazardous. In pushing for bans on safe and medically appropriate abortion services as early as the 12th week of pregnancy, anti-choice forces reject exceptions to protect a woman's health. They aim to restrict access to mifepristone (RU 486), a safe early option for nonsurgical abortion, or take it off the market altogether. They deny public funding for abortion services even when continuing the pregnancy would endanger a woman's health. They put up roadblocks for young women that jeopardize teens' health and can force them to have later-term abortions. They construct barriers for all women with state-ordered biased counseling and mandatory delay require-

FAST FACT

According to the Guttmacher Institute, fewer than 0.3 percent of abortion patients experience a complication that requires hospitalization.

ments that can force women to unnecessarily delay the procedure. With these restrictions in place, women's reproductive health is in serious danger.

The legalization of abortion in the United States led to the near elimination of deaths from the procedure. Between 1973 and 1997, the mortality rate associated with legal abortion procedures declined from 4.1 to 0.6 per 100,000 abortions. The American Medical Association's Council on Scientific Affairs credits the shift from illegal to legal abortion services as an important factor in the decline of the abortion-related death rate after *Roe v. Wade*.

Eighty-eight percent of abortions take place in the first 12 weeks of pregnancy, and nearly 99 percent occur during the first 20 weeks. Earlier abortions are associated with fewer mortality and morbidity risks.

A 1999 study of abortion services worldwide found that abortion-related deaths are rare in countries where the procedure is legal, accessible, and performed early in pregnancy by skilled providers. . . .

Illegal Abortion Endangers Women's Health

It is estimated that before 1973, 1.2 million U.S. women resorted to illegal abortion each year and that unsafe illegal abortions caused as many as 5,000 annual deaths. Not surprisingly, anti-choice activists often deny this reality. They point to lower figures tabulated from death certificates—but their position conveniently ignores several facts. Many deaths from illegal abortion would go unlabeled as such because of careless or casual autopsies, lack of experience and ability of autopsy surgeons, and simply the shame and fear associated with abortion's illegality. According to a 1967 study, illegal abortion was the most common single cause of maternal mortality in California. Doctors who worked in emergency rooms before 1973, and saw first-hand the consequences of illegal abortion, would be in the best position to know. Dr. Louise Thomas, a New York City hospital resident during the late 1960s, summed up the dangers of illegal abortion, remembering the "Monday morning abortion lineup" of the pre-*Roe* period:

> What would happen is that the women would get their paychecks on Friday, Friday night they would go to their abortionist and spend their money on the abortion. Saturday they would start being sick and they would drift in on Sunday or Sunday evening, either hemorrhaging or septic, and they would be lined up outside the operating room to be cleaned out Monday morning. There was a lineup of women on stretchers outside the operating room, so you knew if you were an intern or resident, when you came in Monday morning, that was the first thing you were going to do.

A doctor (right) and patient in an illegal abortion clinic in the 1950s. According to the author, prior to 1973 an estimated five thousand US women died each year from illegal abortions.

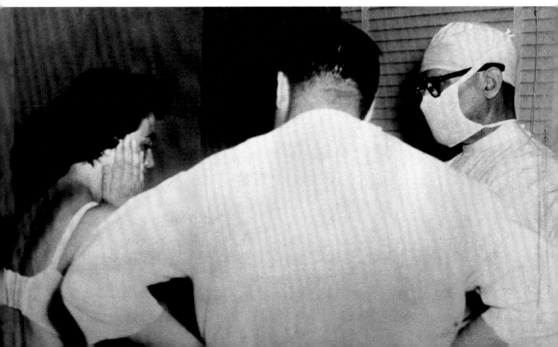

Each year, an estimated 42 million women worldwide obtain abortion services to end unplanned pregnancies; approximately 20 million of them obtain the procedure illegally. According to the World Health Organization, as many as 70,000 of the approximately 600,000 pregnancy-related deaths occurring annually around the world are associated with unsafe abortion. Where abortion is illegal, the risk of complications and maternal mortality is high. In fact, the abortion-related death rate is hundreds of times higher in developing regions, where the procedure is often illegal, than in developed countries.

In 1994, *The New England Journal of Medicine* reported that "[s]erious complications and death from abortion-related infection are almost entirely avoidable. Unfortunately, the prevention of death from abortion remains more a political than a medical problem."

EVALUATING THE AUTHOR'S ARGUMENTS:

In this viewpoint NARAL Pro-Choice America claims that thousands of women died each year from illegal abortions prior to *Roe v. Wade* (1973). What does Human Life International, author of the following viewpoint, say about this figure?

Legal Abortion Has Not Saved Women's Lives

"The evidence shows that death from abortion in the United States was very rare even before abortion was legalized."

Human Life International

In the following viewpoint Human Life International (HLI) contends that the legalization of abortion by the Supreme Court in *Roe v. Wade* in 1973 has not saved women's lives. HLI claims that groups who defend abortion exaggerate the number of women who died from illegal abortion. Rather than saving women's lives, HLI suggests that the existence of legal abortion may actually endanger the lives of women in a variety of ways. As a result, HLI denies the claim that abortion is safer than childbirth. HLI is a Catholic organization that works through missionaries worldwide to defend life from the moment of conception until natural death for all human beings.

AS YOU READ, CONSIDER THE FOLLOWING QUESTIONS:

1. Human Life International (HLI) claims that how many women died from abortions gone wrong in 1972, prior to *Roe v. Wade* (1973)?
2. According to the author, approximately how many pregnant women are murdered each year by men who want them to get abortions?
3. A woman's chances of dying in childbirth or abortion are equal to the chance of what, according to HLI?

1. *Abortion-on-demand has not saved women's lives:* Pro-abortion politicians and groups argue that without easy access to abortion, substantial numbers of women would die through illegal, unregulated, and unsafe "back-alley" abortions. They say that this number of deaths would be greater than the current number of deaths of women caused by the over 1 million legal abortions per year in the United States, and thus that the abortion-on-demand rules imposed by the U.S. Supreme Court in *Roe v. Wade* in 1973 save women's lives. Yet the evidence shows that death from abortion in the United States was very rare before abortion was legalized, and since it has been legalized, maternal mortality rates that had been dropping steadily for decades have leveled out, with the latest reports showing rates higher than any since 1977.

Abortion and Women's Lives

2. *The number of women who died from illegal abortions before* Roe *is greatly exaggerated:* Dr. Bernard Nathanson, a former abortionist who performed tens of thousands of abortions and [is] one of the founders of the National Abortion Rights Action League (NARAL), admitted that he and other NARAL members used to claim that 5,000 to 10,000 women died each year from illegal abortions. He has since admitted that he knew the statistic to be "totally false. . . . But in the 'morality' of our revolution, it was a useful figure, widely accepted, so why go out of our way to correct it with honest statistics?" In 1972, the last year before *Roe v. Wade* was handed down, approximately 90 women died from abortions gone wrong, according to [government health official] Lisa M. Koonin.

3. *Positive trends in maternal health are due to advances in technology:* Progress in medical science in the last few decades, not the widespread practice of legal abortion, has produced declines in maternal deaths. Fortunately, prenatal care, anesthesia technology, antibiotics, and OB-GYN [obstetrics-gynecology] training have all improved since 1972, as Nathanson discussed in "A Pro-Life Medical Response to ACOG's [the American Congress of Obstetricians and Gynecologists'] January 1990 Publication: *Public Health Policy Implications of Abortion*," presented by William F. Colliton, M.D., *et al.* As early as the 1960s, progress in technology had led to the point where abortion was no longer needed to save

Maternal Mortality Rates

Per 100,000 Births

Ireland Poland United States Russia

Abortion Illegal   **Abortion Legal**

Based on data from *UN World Mortality Report*, 2005.

Taken from: National Right to Life Committee, "Does Legalizing Abortion Protect Women's Health?," 2009.

women's lives, if it ever was. Even Dr. Alan Guttmacher, who did more to promote and spread abortion on demand throughout the world than any other individual, commented in 1967, "Today it is possible for almost any patient to be brought through pregnancy alive, unless she suffers from a fatal disease such as cancer or leukemia, and if so, abortion would be unlikely to prolong, much less save the life." Former surgeon general of the United States Dr. C. Everett Koop said, "The life-of-the-mother argument surfaces in every debate concerning abortion. The fact of the matter is that abortion as a necessity to save the life of the mother is so rare as to be non-existent."

4. *Legalized abortion has led to more maternal deaths by cultural means.* While total deaths due to abortionist incompetence have probably decreased in the United States thanks to better technology and training, maternal deaths due to other abortion-related causes have increased dramatically. At least three major studies have shown that the most common cause of fatalities among pregnant women is murder, and statistics show that almost one-third of these are due to men who kill their wives or girlfriends because they refuse to get an abortion. This amounts to 30 to 50 murders a year.

The author maintains that maternal health has improved due to technological advances in medicine [that may be used apart from abortion, as in the examination pictured here], not because abortion has been legalized.

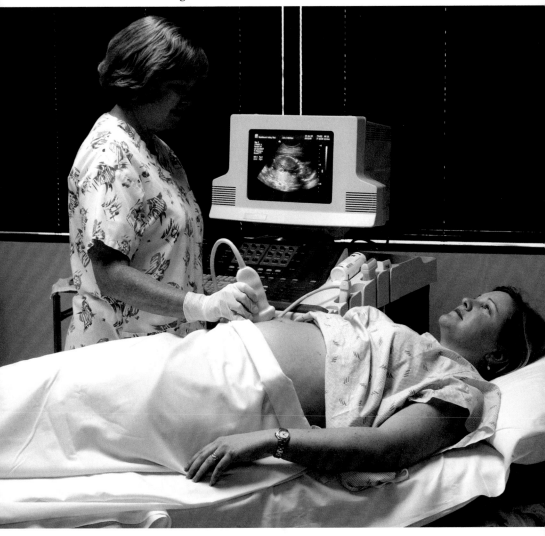

Abortion Worldwide

5. *Global abortion-related deaths are also exaggerated*: Pro-abortion groups exaggerate the number of women who die of illegal abortion complications around the world. The most common figures used are 78,000; 200,000; and half a million annually. A review of the sources for these figures reveals that they do not have solid evidence behind them. The actual number is probably closer to 2,000 deaths world-wide annually due to illegal abortions.

6. *Maternal death rates are lower where abortion is outlawed*: In fact, countries [having] strict limits on abortion—and where laws against abortion are enforced—usually have much lower maternal mortality rates than those nations with legal and common abortion. According to the United Nations Population Division in its *World Mortality Report: 2005,* Ireland and Poland, countries where abortion is highly restricted, have rates of 5 per 100,000 and 13 per 100,000 births, respectively; the United States has a rate of 17 per 100,000; and Russia, with one of the world's highest abortion rates, has 67 per 100,000 births. Many developing countries where abortion is illegal have high maternal death rates due to poverty, lack of education, grossly inadequate medical facilities and other factors. When international development tries to address these factors, they enjoy support from pro-life groups, but claims that legalized abortion actually improves women's health are specious at best once evidence is considered closely. Further, Chile, which is considered a developing nation and has heavily restricted abortion since the 1980s, has actually seen a dramatic decrease in maternal mortality. The primary author of a study released in early 2010 attributes the better health outcomes for mothers who give birth to improvements such as "highly trained personnel, the construction of many primary health centers and the increase of schooling of the population."

> **FAST FACT**
>
> The Centers for Disease Control and Prevention reported that six deaths in the United States in 2006 (the latest year available as of 2011) were related to legal abortion.

Legal Abortion Results in a Culture of Death

George Neumayr

"Legal abortion since Roe hasn't eliminated the horrors of the 'back alley' but brought them to Main Street."

In the following viewpoint George Neumayr claims that the protection of a woman's right to abortion in *Roe v. Wade* (1973) has resulted in a callous abortion culture that undervalues life. Neumayr claims that the recent indictment of a Pennsylvania late-term abortionist for infanticide illustrates the grisly nature of legal abortion. He claims that the support for late-term abortions by abortion-rights advocates shows how the *Roe*-dominated culture has resulted in a blatant disregard for life. Neumayr is editor of *Catholic World Report*.

AS YOU READ, CONSIDER THE FOLLOWING QUESTIONS:

1. The author charges that abortion, rather than being safe and rare, is what?
2. The author claims that abortion-rights advocates who denounce the actions of Kermit Gosnell show disgust based not on morality but on what?
3. According to Neumayr, Gosnell expressed puzzlement at what charge?

Shortly before the anniversary of the *Roe v. Wade* [1973] decision in January [2011], a grand jury in Pennsylvania charged long-time Philadelphia abortionist Kermit Gosnell with seven acts of infanticide and the killing of one adult—a vivid illustration of the unfolding civilizational damage and cheapening of life that *Roe* continues to cause.

The Culture of Legal Abortion

Abortion-rights advocates were eager to dismiss the story as an aberration and return to their nostalgic remembrances of the *Roe* ruling. But in truth the indictment throws awful light on the inevitable consequences of *Roe*'s pervasive abortion culture. Contrary to the popular slogan, abortion is not "safe" and "rare" in America but unsafe and frequent, resulting in cases like this one. Legal abortion since *Roe* hasn't eliminated the horrors of the "back alley" but brought them to Main Street. Gosnell's callousness is just a more explicit and obvious example of a disregard for life that exists at more "respectable" abortion clinics across the country.

Though *Roe* technically permits some restrictions on abortion, the ethos behind it has gradually weakened those restrictions in practice; the "right to choose" now means for many in the abortion industry the right to choose every type of abortion, including late-term ones that border on or sometimes become infanticide. The lax oversight of late-term abortionists like Gosnell is not an accident; it is an outgrowth of the "sacred" space and respect accorded to those who seek and provide abortion under a *Roe*-dominated culture.

The Gosnell case, as the Pennsylvania grand jury noted, did not happen in an ideological vacuum. According to its report, an abortion-rights atmosphere in Pennsylvania explains the state's unwillingness to investigate abortion clinics like his: "[t]he Pennsylvania Department of Health abruptly decided, for political reasons, to stop inspecting abortion clinics at all. The politics in question were not anti-abortion, but pro. With the change of administration from Governor [Bob] Casey to Governor [Tom] Ridge, officials concluded that inspections would be 'putting a barrier up to women' seeking abortions. Even nail salons in Pennsylvania are monitored more closely for client safety."

A Late-Term Abortionist

A known figure in the abortion industry, Gosnell killed countless unborn children for more than three decades, earning sometimes more than a million dollars a year. The grand jury report found that Gosnell "regularly and illegally delivered live, viable babies in the third trimester of pregnancy—and then murdered these newborns by severing their spinal cords with scissors." Investigators found remains of fetuses scattered throughout his clinic, with some even stored in the staff refrigerator. Many people in Philadelphia knew about this, including a representative from the National Abortion Federation, but no one initiated a state investigation. What finally stopped Gosnell was a prescription drug raid completely unrelated to abortion.

In a time when late-term abortionists are sometimes romanticized by pro-choicers as fearlessly defiant providers of a stigmatized but needed service, in a time when pro-choicers worry far more about what is said inside crisis pregnancy centers than what is done inside abortion clinics, figures like Gosnell are bound to exist.

Some abortion-rights advocates have agreed that the horrors contained within his clinic should lead to better oversight of abortion providers. But the case has not led them to consider the grisly nature of abortion itself. Whatever disgust they feel for Gosnell is more aesthetic than moral, more directed at his treatment of female patients than unborn children.

The Views of Abortion-Rights Advocates

Indeed, many abortion-rights advocates defend the late-term abortions that largely defined his practice. The journalist William Saletan has noted that leading "reproductive rights activists" in recent times

Pictured here is the Women's Medical Society in Philadelphia, where Dr. Kermit Gosnell performed late-term abortions. He was eventually charged with seven acts of infanticide and the death of one adult.

have made explicit their support for abortions at any stage. "Is there anything qualitatively different about a fetus at, say, 28 weeks that gives it a morally different status to a fetus at 18 weeks or even eight weeks?" Ann Furedi, chief executive of the British Pregnancy Advisory Service, has asked. "Why should we assume later abortions are 'bad'—or, at least, 'more wrong' than early ones?"

Abortion-rights advocates Steph Herold and Susan Yanow say: "Women have no obligation to make a decision as soon as they possibly can. The only obligation women have is to take the time they need to make the decision that is right for them. Don't we believe that women are moral decision makers, and carefully consider their options when faced with an unwanted pregnancy?"

Saletan quotes Marge Berer, editor of *Reproductive Health Matters*, as saying that "an abortion provider must never pass judgment on the validity of a woman's need for an abortion," but "should act as technicians with a clinical skill to offer." She concludes that "anyone who thinks they have the right to refuse even one woman an abortion can't continue to claim they are pro-choice."

Kermit Gosnell would certainly agree. He took any case that came to him. He offered his clinical skill to one and all. And he performed the late abortions that pro-choicers urged [President] George W. Bush not to ban. It is no wonder that at his bail hearing Gosnell expressed puzzlement not to the charge of killing an adult patient but to the charge of killing seven babies. "Is it possible you could explain the seven counts?" he asked. In a *Roe*-ravaged culture, the answer to his question is not very clear.

EVALUATING THE AUTHOR'S ARGUMENTS:

In this viewpoint George Neumayr reports that the late-term abortion provider Kermit Gosnell was charged with murder, or infanticide, for seven abortions. Relying on the reasoning of one of the previous authors in this volume, give one reason in favor of the idea that the killing of an unborn fetus can never be murder.

Opponents of Abortion Are Creating a Culture of Terror

Melissa Harris-Perry

"The anti-choice community operates with a totalitarian impulse that generates a culture of terror rather than a culture of life."

In the following viewpoint Melissa Harris-Perry argues that the murder of abortion doctor George Tiller was an act of terrorism, which she claims is an outgrowth of the culture of terror created by the anti-choice community. Harris-Perry contends that the opponents of legal abortion have used the strategy of isolating, dividing, and dehumanizing women in order to instill terror. She proposes that women share their personal narratives in order to counteract this terrorism. Harris-Perry is a professor of political science at Tulane University, where she is founding director of the Project on Gender, Race, and Politics in the South.

I believe the murder of [abortion provider] George Tiller was an
act of domestic terrorism whose aim was not only to assassinate
a single man, but also to frighten a generation of doctors and to
shame and terrify women and families who are making difficult
choices. While the murderous rage of Tiller's assassin is not representative of the broader anti-choice movement, I believe that the anti-
choice community operates with a totalitarian impulse that generates
a culture of terror rather than a culture of life.

HOMEGROWN TERRORIST

"Homegrown terrorist," cartoon by RJ Matson, *The St. Louis Post-Dispatch*, June 3, 2009, and
CagleCartoons.com. Copyright © 2009 by RJ Matson and CagleCartoons.com. All rights reserved.
Reproduced by permission.

A Dehumanizing Strategy

[German philosopher] Hannah Arendt suggested that totalitarians generate terror in part by cultivating profound loneliness among their targets. Loneliness locks human beings in isolation and hampers discourse, connection, and shared experience. When we believe we are alone and misunderstood we cannot form the bonds necessary to organize and resist. There are few experiences more lonely and isolating than facing an unintended pregnancy or facing the need to terminate a desired pregnancy in order to protect maternal health. The anti-choice discourse labels the

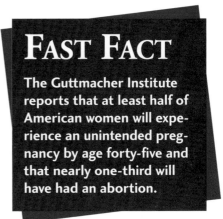

women and families who chose abortion "baby killers." It is a strategy that dehumanizes these women and the doctors who care for them.

The strategy is effective because abortion still carries tremendous social shame in addition to its personal psychological burden. Activists for reproductive rights have a hard time convincing women and families who have terminated to be part of a movement that protects the right to terminate. Many understandably prefer not to be publicly associated with the stigma and potential violence that comes with standing up for choice.

The Difference Privilege Makes

It also works because abortion, like all American healthcare, is profoundly shaped by structures of privilege and access. Wealthy women in urban areas with private insurance who have long-term relationships with physicians have more access to privacy and to termination services than do other women. Poor women, teenagers, rural women, women suffering with domestic violence, and uninsured women are much more likely to have to risk some level of public scrutiny of their decision to seek an abortion. They cannot request a D&C [dilatation and curettage, a gynecological surgical procedure that can be used as an abortion method] from their private provider, they must seek out a clinic. Even during the dark years of back alley abortions when all women seeking abortion were at risk, it was the most vulnerable women who carried the heaviest burden of infection, illness, and death.

Because women of privilege can keep their termination choices private while vulnerable women are exposed to public shaming, it becomes easier to believe that only those "other" women and "bad" women choose abortion. Telling our stories is part of counteracting the terrorism that seeks to divide, shame, and even murder to impose its own worldview. Nurturing a sense of commonality and shared experience reduces the power of terror. Women need realistic understandings of how many women grapple with these choices and the different ways they come to make a decision. Such information is shockingly difficult to access. Often women must wade through disgusting, painful, and misleading "information" about abortion just to get basic medical advice. While there are political, judicial, and structural aspects to this issue, I want to also make an appeal for the power of our personal narratives to fight back against anti-choice terrorism

The Power of Personal Narratives

Forty years ago my mother was part of the movement of individuals who helped desperate women find safe ways to terminate their pregnancies. This network provided safe houses, transportation, and follow-up support for women who had to cross state lines to obtain abortions. She was willing to risk her life and livelihood to protect women's reproductive choices.

Nearly twenty years ago my older sister was diagnosed with cancer during the second trimester of her pregnancy. Her religious commitments led her to refuse her doctor's advice to terminate. She risked her life to ensure that she would not have an abortion. She and my niece are both healthy.

When we were 14-year-old high school freshmen, my friend decided to have the baby of a boy she'd had sex with only once. It changed her life forever, but she graduated from school and made a life for herself and daughter. In my twenties I stood by dear friends who simply could not afford emotionally or financially to carry their pregnancies to term. Their decisions to seek abortions were difficult and painful, but they faced them courageously.

Fire investigators work the crime scene at an abortion clinic in Nebraska. The antiabortion movement has been responsible for attacks like this one on a number of abortion clinics and individual doctors.

I'm a 35-year-old, educated, black, divorced mother. Like so many other women my age I have faced my own tough reproductive choices. I've had a child, an abortion, and hysterectomy. I love and respect women who have chosen many different paths. Their stories and my own are part of the reason that I am a committed supporter of reproductive rights.

The murder of George Tiller is personal to me. It is not just a matter of politics or policy. I am an aunt to three teenage girls and the mother to a daughter. It is critical to me that their health, safety, and choices are protected.

EVALUATING THE AUTHOR'S ARGUMENTS:

In this viewpoint Melissa Harris-Perry argues that the pro-life community does not promote a culture of life but actually promotes a culture of terror. Identify a pro-life author in this volume that you believe could best refute Harris-Perry on this point. Explain your choice.

Facts About Abortion

Editor's note: These facts can be used in reports or papers to reinforce or add credibility when making important points or claims.

The Legal Status of Abortion
Worldwide
- According to the Center for Reproductive Rights, seventy countries —representing more than 60 percent of the world's population— permit abortion on broad grounds.

United States
- In the 1973 case of *Roe v. Wade*, the US Supreme Court ruled that women have a constitutionally protected right to abortion in the early stages of pregnancy.
- In the 1992 case *of Planned Parenthood v. Casey*, the Supreme Court ruled that states may enact certain restrictions on abortion in the early stages of pregnancy, including informed consent requirements, parental consent requirements, and a mandatory twenty-four-hour waiting period.
- Thirty-four states require that women receive counseling before an abortion is performed to establish informed consent.
- Twenty-two states require parental consent, sixteen states require parental notice, and five states require both parental consent and parental notice for a minor's abortion.
- Twenty-five states require a waiting period between counseling and obtaining an abortion, usually twenty-four hours.
- In 2007 the US Supreme Court upheld the Partial Birth Abortion Ban Act, which bans a particular abortion method formerly used in the second and third trimesters (more than three months into a pregnancy).

Abortion Statistics in the United States
The following statistics are provided by the Guttmacher Institute:
- From 1973 through 2008, nearly 50 million legal abortions were performed.

- Each year, 2 percent of women aged fifteen to forty-four have an abortion.
- Twenty-two percent of all pregnancies end in abortion.
- Thirty percent of American women will have had an abortion by age forty-five.
- More than half of all abortions are obtained by women in their twenties, and 18 percent of abortions are obtained by teenagers.
- Women who have never married and are not living with a partner account for 45 percent of all abortions.
- Forty-two percent of women who have abortions have incomes below the federal poverty level.
- Fifty-four percent of women who have abortions became pregnant while using birth control.

Based on surveillance of abortion in its most recent year studied, 2007, the Centers for Disease Control and Prevention cites the following statistics:

- Sixty-two percent of abortions were performed at eight weeks' gestation or earlier, and 92 percent were performed at thirteen weeks or earlier.
- Among the abortions performed at eight weeks or earlier, 20 percent were nonsurgical, medical abortions using a prescribed medicine.
- From 1973 to 2006, 383 women died from complications related to legal abortions.

Public Opinion on Abortion in the United States

A Gallup poll in July 2011 gathered the following statistics:

- Twenty-six percent of respondents believed abortion should be legal under any circumstances; 51 percent believed abortion should be legal only under certain circumstances, and 20 percent believe abortion should be illegal in all circumstances.
- Eighty-seven percent favored a law requiring doctors to inform women about possible risks of abortion before performing the procedure, whereas 11 percent opposed such a law.
- Fifty percent favored a law requiring that a woman seeking an abortion be shown an ultrasound image of her fetus at least twenty-four hours before the procedure, whereas 46 percent opposed such a law.

- Seventy-one percent favored a law requiring parental consent for a minor to get an abortion, whereas 27 percent opposed such a law.
- Sixty-nine percent favored a law requiring a twenty-four-hour waiting period to get an abortion, whereas 28 percent opposed such a law.
- Fifty-seven percent opposed a law prohibiting health clinics that provide abortion services from receiving any federal funds, whereas 40 percent favored such a law.
- Forty-seven percent of those polled considered themselves pro-choice, and 47 percent considered themselves pro-life.

A poll by CBS News and the *New York Times* conducted in 2010 produced the following result:

- Fifty-eight percent of respondents said they believed the Supreme Court's decision in *Roe v. Wade* (1973) was a good one, whereas 34 percent said it was a bad decision.

Organizations to Contact

The editors have compiled the following list of organizations concerned with the issues debated in this book. The descriptions are derived from materials provided by the organizations. All have publications or information available for interested readers. The list was compiled on the date of publication of the present volume; the information provided here may change. Be aware that many organizations take several weeks or longer to respond to inquiries, so allow as much time as possible for the receipt of requested materials.

Advocates for Youth
2000 M St. NW, Ste. 750, Washington, DC 20036
(202) 419-3420
fax: (202) 419-1448
website: www.advocatesforyouth.org

Advocates for Youth is an organization that works both in the United States and in developing countries with a sole focus on adolescent reproductive and sexual health. The organization champions efforts that help young people make informed and responsible decisions about their reproductive and sexual health through its core values of rights, respect, and responsibility. Advocates for Youth publishes numerous informational essays available at its website, including "Adolescents and Abortion."

American Center for Law and Justice (ACLJ)
PO Box 90555, Washington, DC 20090-0555
(800) 296-4529
website: www.aclj.org

The ACLJ is dedicated to the ideal that religious freedom and freedom of speech are inalienable, God-given rights. The ACLJ has participated in numerous cases before the US Supreme Court, federal courts of appeals, federal district courts, and various state courts regarding freedom of religion and freedom of speech. The ACLJ has numerous memos and position papers available at its website, including the memo "Federal Healthcare Funding and Abortion."

American Civil Liberties Union (ACLU)
125 Broad St., 18th Fl., New York, NY 10004
(212) 549-2500
e-mail: infoaclu@aclu.org
website: www.aclu.org

The ACLU is a national organization that works to defend Americans' civil rights as guaranteed in the US Constitution. The ACLU's Reproductive Freedom Project works in courts, legislatures, and communities to protect everyone's right to make informed decisions free from government interference about whether and when to become a parent. The ACLU publishes the semiannual newsletter *Civil Liberties Alert,* as well as briefing papers, including "Reproductive Rights in the Courts: 2010."

American Life League (ALL)
PO Box 1350, Stafford, VA 22555
(540) 659-4171
fax: (540) 659-2586
website: www.all.org

ALL is a Catholic organization that opposes abortion. It sponsors a number of outreach efforts designed to focus attention on individual pro-life concerns. ALL provides brochures, videos, and newsletters at its website, including the brochure "A Person's a Person, No Matter How Small."

Catholics for Choice (CFC)
1436 U St. NW, Ste. 301, Washington, DC 20009-3997
(202) 986-6093
fax: (202) 332-7995
e-mail: cfc@catholicsforchoice.org
website: www.catholicsforchoice.org

The CFC is a Catholic organization that supports a woman's moral and legal right to follow her conscience in matters of sexuality and reproductive health. The organization works in the United States and internationally to ensure that all people have access to safe and affordable reproductive health care. The CFC publishes *Conscience* magazine and articles including "In Good Conscience: Respecting the Beliefs of Health-Care Providers and the Needs of Patients."

Center for Reproductive Rights

120 Wall St., New York, NY 10005
(917) 637-3600
fax: (917) 637-3666
e-mail: info@reprorights.org
website: www.reproductiverights.org

The Center for Reproductive Rights is a global legal advocacy organization dedicated to reproductive rights. The center uses the law to advance reproductive freedom as a fundamental human right that all governments are legally obligated to protect, respect, and fulfill. The center publishes articles, reports, and briefing papers, among which is the article "Parental Involvement Laws."

Concerned Women for America (CWA)

1015 Fifteenth St. NW, Ste. 1100, Washington, DC 20005
(202) 488-7000
fax: (202) 488-0806
website: www.cwfa.org

The CWA is a public policy women's organization that has the goal of bringing biblical principles into all levels of public policy. The CWA focuses on promoting biblical values on six core issues—family, sanctity of human life, education, pornography, religious liberty, and national sovereignty—through prayer, education, and social influence. Among the brochures, fact sheets, and articles available on the organization's website is "It's Time to Reject *Roe v. Wade* as Invincible Precedent."

Feminists for Life of America

PO Box 320667, Alexandria, VA 22320
e-mail: info@feministsforlife.org
website: www.feministsforlife.org

Feminists for Life of America is a nonsectarian, nonpartisan organization that seeks to eliminate the root causes that drive women to abortion. The organization provides practical resources and support shaped by feminism to help women to avoid abortion. Feminists for Life of America publishes the *American Feminist* and articles such as "Women Deserve Better than Abortion."

Guttmacher Institute
125 Maiden Ln., 7th Fl., New York, NY 10038
(800) 355-0244
fax: (212) 248-1951
website: www.guttmacher.org

The Guttmacher Institute works to advance sexual and reproductive health worldwide through an interrelated program of social science research, public education, and policy analysis. The institute collects and analyzes scientific evidence to make a difference in policies, programs, and medical practice. The institute publishes the *Guttmacher Policy Review*, available at its website, and other publications, including the monthly *State Policies in Brief,* which provides information on legislative and judicial actions affecting reproductive health, such as "An Overview of Minors' Consent Laws."

Human Life Foundation, Inc.
353 Lexington Ave., Ste. 802, New York, NY 10016
website: www.humanlifereview.com

The Human Life Foundation is a nonprofit corporation with the goal of promoting alternatives to abortion. The organization works to encourage such alternatives through educational and charitable means. The foundation publishes the *Human Life Review*, a quarterly journal that focuses on abortion and other life issues.

Human Life International (HLI)
4 Family Life Ln., Front Royal, VA 22630
(800) 549-5433
fax: (540) 622-6247
e-mail: hli@hli.org
website: www.hli.org

The HLI is an international pro-life organization that opposes abortion. With affiliates and associates in over a hundred countries, the HLI trains, organizes, and equips pro-life leaders around the world. The HLI publishes the monthly newsletters *Mission Report* and *Front-Lines,* as well as *Pro-Life Talking Points,* among which is "Exceptions: Is Abortion Ever Permissible?"

NARAL Pro-Choice America

1156 Fifteenth St. NW, Ste. 700, Washington, DC 20005
(202) 973-3000
fax: (202) 973-3096
website: www.naral.org

NARAL Pro-Choice America advocates for privacy and a woman's right to choose abortion. NARAL works to elect pro-choice candidates, lobbies Congress to protect reproductive rights, and monitors state and federal activity in the courts related to reproductive rights. The organization publishes numerous fact sheets, including "Abortion Funding Restrictions Threaten Women's Health."

National Right to Life Committee (NRLC)

512 Tenth St. NW, Washington, DC 20004
(202) 626-8800
e-mail: nrlc@nrlc.org
website: www.nrlc.org

The NRLC was established after the US Supreme Court decision in *Roe v. Wade* (1973), with the goal of repealing the right to abortion. It works toward legislative reform at the national level to restrict abortion. The committee publishes a monthly newspaper, the *National Right to Life News,* and several fact sheets, such as "Teens and Abortion: Why Parents Should Know."

Planned Parenthood Federation of America

434 W. Thirty-Third St., New York, NY 10001
(212) 541-7800
fax: (212) 245-1845
website: www.plannedparenthood.org

Planned Parenthood is a sexual and reproductive health care provider and advocate. The organization works to improve women's health and safety, prevent unintended pregnancies, and advance the right and ability of individuals and families to make informed and responsible choices. At its website, Planned Parenthood offers information about birth control, as well as position papers, such as "Affordable Birth Control and Other Preventative Care."

Religious Coalition for Reproductive Choice
1413 K St. NW, 14th Fl., Washington, DC 20005
(202) 628-7700
fax: (202) 628-7716
e-mail: info@rcrc.org
website: www.rcrc.org

The Religious Coalition for Reproductive Choice is composed of national organizations from major faiths and traditions and religiously affiliated and independent religious organizations that support reproductive choice and religious freedom. The coalition uses education and advocacy to give voice to the reproductive issues of people of color, those living in poverty, and other underserved populations. The coalition publishes a newsletter, *Faith & Choices*, and various articles, such as "Believe It: Religious Americans Are Pro-choice."

Books

Ainsworth, Scott, and Thad E. Hall. *Abortion Politics in Congress: Strategic Incrementalism and Policy Change.* New York: Cambridge University Press, 2011. Examines how legislators have juggled their passions over abortion, looking at how both external and internal factors shape abortion policy.

Baumgardner, Jennifer. *Abortion & Life.* New York: Akashic, 2008. Explores the issue of abortion through photographs of women who have had abortions and their testimonials explaining why they made the choice they did.

Beckwith, Francis J. *Defending Life: A Moral and Legal Case Against Abortion Choice.* New York: Cambridge University Press, 2007. Defends the pro-life position on abortion from a moral, scientific, legal, and political perspective, offering critical analysis of *Roe v. Wade* and other court decisions.

Everhard, Matthew. *Abortion: The Evangelical Perspective.* North Richland Hills, TX: BIBAL, 2007. Surveys the history of Christian teaching on abortion, identifying six biblical propositions that form the basis of an evangelical position against abortion.

Hull, N.E.H., and Peter Charles Hoffer. Roe v. Wade: *The Abortion Rights Controversy in American History.* Lawrence: University Press of Kansas, 2010. Highlights abortion's historical background, the core issues of *Roe v. Wade* (1973), and subsequent challenges to it in *Webster v. Reproductive Services* (1989) and *Casey v. Planned Parenthood* (1992).

Joffe, Carole. *Dispatches from the Abortion Wars: The Costs of Fanaticism to Doctors, Patients, and the Rest of Us.* Boston: Beacon, 2009. Argues that a pervasive stigma cultivated by the religious right operates to maintain barriers to access by shaming women and marginalizing abortion providers.

Kaczor, Christopher. *The Ethics of Abortion: Women's Rights, Human Life, and the Question of Justice.* New York: Routledge, 2011. Argues for the view that all abortions are morally wrong and that doctors and nurses who object to abortion should not be forced to act against their consciences.

Lee, Patrick. *Abortion & Unborn Human Life.* 2nd ed. Washington, DC: Catholic University of America Press, 2010. Argues that unborn human beings have inherent dignity and are subjects of basic rights from the moment of fertilization.

Linton, Paul Benjamin. *Abortion Under State Constitutions: A State-by-State Analysis.* Durham, NC: Carolina Academic Press, 2008. Explores arguments for and against the recognition of abortion as a state constitutional right.

Macleod, Catriona. *Adolescence, Pregnancy, and Abortion: Constructing a Threat of Degeneration.* New York: Routledge, 2010. Argues that the negativity surrounding teenage pregnancy and abortion is underpinned by a particular understanding of adolescence.

Shapiro, Ian, ed. *Abortion: The Supreme Court Decisions, 1965–2007.* Indianapolis: Hackett, 2007. Provides all of the major Supreme Court decisions on abortion, including many majority, dissenting, and plurality opinions.

Singular, Stephen. *The Wichita Divide: The Murder of Dr. George Tiller and the Battle over Abortion.* New York: St. Martin's, 2011. Gives an in-depth account of the life and death of a controversial doctor and the debate that sparked his assassination.

Slack, James D. *Abortion, Execution, and the Consequences of Taking Life.* New Brunswick, NJ: Transaction, 2011. Explores the relationship between public morality and personal action in the American political community regarding the issues of abortion and capital punishment.

Stevens, John V., Sr. *The Abortion Controversy: Will a Free America Survive? Will You?* Sun City, AZ: Founders Freedom, 2008. Investigates the arguments for and against abortion, arguing that the abortion issue is part of a larger crisis threatening the very survival of America.

Tooley, Michael, Celia Wolf-Devine, Philip E. Devine, and Alison M. Jaggar. *Abortion: Three Perspectives.* New York: Oxford University Press, 2009. Four authors debate three different approaches to the abortion issue: the liberal approach, the communitarian approach, and the feminist approach.

Periodicals and Internet Sources

Allott, Daniel, and Matt Bowman. "The Right of Conscience in the Age of Obama: It Can No Longer Be Taken for Granted," *American Spectator*, November 2009.

Bachmann, Michele. "Is No Girl Too Young for Plan B?," Townhall.com, April 23, 2009. www.townhall.com.

Balko, Radley. "Getting Beyond *Roe:* Why Returning Abortion to the States Is a Good Idea," *Reason*, August/September 2007.

Bandow, Doug. "The Consequences of the Culture of Death," *American Spectator*, June 29, 2009.

Bandow, Doug. "Moral Challenges of Abortion," *Korea Times*, September 13, 2009.

Bastien, Richard. "The Flawed Logic of the Pro-choice Stance," *Catholic Insight*, June 2008.

Bauer, Gary. "The Abortion Debate Needs to Include the Forgotten Fathers," *Christian Science Monitor*, June 18, 2010.

Bauer, Gary, and Star Parker. "A Dream Unfulfilled: *Roe v. Wade* Has Played a Big Role in the Devastation of the African American Community," *Weekly Standard*, January 21, 2009.

Beenfeldt, Christian. "Abortion Is Not Murder: So-Called 'Pro-Life Movement' Is Anti-Human," *Capitalism*, November 11, 2006.

Buckley, William F., Jr. "Questions of Life and Death," *National Review*, December 31, 2007.

Campbell, Colleen Carroll. "A Reality Check Before an Abortion," *St. Louis (MO) Post-Dispatch*, May 6, 2010.

Clark, Thomas W. "Faith in Hiding: Are There Secular Grounds for Banning Abortion?," *Humanist*, July/August 2007.

Cohen, Susan A. "Abortion and Women of Color: The Bigger Picture," *Guttmacher Policy Review*, Summer 2008.

Cohen, Susan A. "Facts and Consequences: Legality, Incidence, and Safety of Abortion Worldwide," *Guttmacher Policy Review*, Fall 2009.

Derbyshire, Stuart W.G. "Fetal Pain?," *Conscience*, Fall 2010.

Dresser, Rebecca. "Protecting Women from Their Abortion Choices," *Hastings Center Report*, November/December 2007.

D'Souza, Dinesh. "Sex, Lies, and Abortion: It's Time to Get to the Bottom of the Great National Tragedy," *Christianity Today*, September 2009.

Dworkin, Ronald. "The Court and Abortion: Worse than You Think," *New York Review of Books*, May 31, 2007.

Epstein, Alex. "The Religious Right's Culture of Living Death," *Coeur d'Alene (ID) Press*, April 22, 2007.

Frantz, Karen. "The Politics of Personhood," *Humanist*, November/December 2008.

Goldstein, Dana. "A 'Uniquely American' Abortion Debate," *American Prospect*, July 28, 2009.

Gray, Stephen. "The Evil of 'Choice,'" *Catholic Insight*, March 2008.

Hendrix, Joey. "Abortions for Soldiers at US Military Bases?," *Christian Science Monitor*, July 21, 2010.

Kiourkas, Iliana. "At the Intersection of Abortion Rights and Antichoice: A Quiet Street Corner Exemplifies an Intense Dispute," *Women's Health Activist*, November/December 2010.

Kissling, Frances, and Kate Michelman. "Abortion's Battle of Messages," *Los Angeles Times*, January 22, 2008.

Kotz, Deborah. "Should the Government Pay for Abortions?," *US News and World Report*, December 8, 2008.

Krajacic, Zach. "Serious About Reducing Abortion? Make Women See an Ultrasound of the Procedure," *Christian Science Monitor*, January 7, 2010.

Lemieux, Scott. "Bypassing Young Women's Abortion Rights," *American Prospect*, August 17, 2007.

Lithwick, Dahlia. "The Abortion Wars Get Technical," *Newsweek*, December 15, 2008.

Lott, John R., Jr. "Abortion and Crime: One Has an Effect on the Other, but It May Not Be the Effect You Think," *National Review*, August 13, 2007.

Love, Rozalyn Farmer. "Why I Plan to Emulate Dr. George Tiller," *Atlanta Journal-Constitution*, June 9, 2009.

Marcus, Ruth. "Abortion's New Battleground," *Newsweek*, December 7, 2009.

Monahan, Jeanne. "Nix Abortion Funding," *Washington Times*, January 26, 2010.

Moore, Steven C. "A Tragic Inheritance: A Personal Perspective on the Abortion Debate," *America*, February 16, 2009.

New, Michael J. "A Parental-Involvement Opportunity," *National Review*, September 16, 2008.

New York Times. "More than Onerous," March 15, 2010.

O'Brien, Jon. "Reducing the Need for Abortion: Honest Effort or Ideological Dodge?," *Conscience,* Spring 2009.

Schulman, Sam. "Honor Killing, American-Style: What Science and *Roe v. Wade* Made Possible Has Become Virtually Mandatory Among Our Self-Anointed Elites," *Weekly Standard,* April 13, 2009.

Senior, Jennifer. "The Abortion Distortion: Just How Pro-choice Is America, Really?," *New York,* December 7, 2009.

Telzrow, Michael E. "Before *Roe v. Wade,*" *New American,* January 21, 2008.

Thiessen, Marc A. "Bringing Humanity Back to the Abortion Debate," *Washington Post,* April 19, 2010.

Unger, Stephen. "Why Abortion Is NOT Murder," OpEdNews.com, November 14, 2008. www.opednews.com.

Van Biema, David. "America Without *Roe v. Wade,*" *Time,* September 25, 2008.

Vuoto, Grace. "Sliding Toward Infanticide: Obama Policy Renders All Americans Complicit in Killing of the Unborn," *Washington Times,* August 6, 2010.

Will, George F. "Golly, What Did Jon Do?," *Newsweek,* January 29, 2007.

Willcox, Jennifer N. "Do Health Providers Have 'Right to Refuse'?," *Connecticut Law Tribune,* May 11, 2009.

Yanow, Susan. "The Need for Second-Trimester Abortion Advocacy," *Conscience,* Spring 2009.

Websites

Centers for Disease Control and Prevention (CDC) (www.cdc.gov). This website contains data and statistics from the CDC's Abortion Surveillance System.

eMedicineHealth (www.emedicinehealth.com). Owned and operated by WebMD, this website includes information about the history of abortion and abortion laws in the United States, information on different types of abortion, and statistics.

US Census Bureau (www.census.gov). This website contains information from the National Data Book, which contains statistics on abortions in the United States.

Index

Picture Credits

© AP Images, 46
© AP Images/J. Scott Applewhite, 92
© AP Images/Manuel Balce Ceneta, 11
© AP Images/Chuck France, 72
© AP Images/Nati Harnik, 121
© AP Images/Danny Johnston, 77
© AP Images/New Bern Sun Journal, Byron Holland, 15
© AP Images/Matt Rourke, 115
© AP Images/Jeff Tuttle, 60
© Bettmann/Corbis, 104
© Cris Bouroncle/AFP/Getty Images, 33
© Tim Boyles/Getty Images, 25
© CNP/Ron Sachs/Getty Images, 56
© Scott J. Ferrell/Congressional Quarterly/Getty Images, 99
Gale/Cengage Learning, 14, 27, 31, 44, 55, 62, 66, 73, 79, 84, 93, 98, 108
© Spencer Grant/Photo Researchers, Inc., 109
© Brendan Hoffman/Getty Images, 87
© Mike Hutmacher/Wichita Eagle/MCT via Getty Images, 20
© Bettye Lane/Photo researchers, Inc., 89
© Newsmakers/Getty Images, 68
© 3D4Medical/Photo Researchers, Inc., 37
© Tom Williams/Roll Call/Getty Images, 49